soulsister

trust

Tamie Vervoorn

Regal

Ventura, California, U.S.A.

Gospel Light is a Christian publisher dedicated to serving the local church. We believe God's vision for Gospel Light is to provide church leaders with biblical, user-friendly materials that will help them evangelize, disciple and minister to children, youth and families.

It is our prayer that this Gospel Light resource will help you discover biblical truth for your own life and help you minister to youth. May God richly bless you.

For a free catalog of resources from Gospel Light, please contact your Christian supplier or contact us at 1-800-4-GOSPEL *or* www.gospellight.com.

PUBLISHING STAFF
Dr. Elmer L. Towns, Senior Consulting Publisher • **Bruce Barbour,** Editorial Director • **Alex Field,** Acquisition Editor • **Bayard Taylor, M.Div.,** Senior Editor, Biblical and Theological Issues

© 2006 Gospel Light
All rights reserved.
Printed in the U.S.A.

Library of Congress Cataloging-in-Publication Data
Vervoorn, Tamie.
 Soul sister : trust / Tamie Vervoorn.
     p. cm.
 ISBN 0-8307-4296-4 (trade paper)
 1. Teenage girls—Religious life. 2. Trust in God. 3. Spirituality. I. Title.
 BV4551.3.V47 2006
 248.8'33—dc22

2006025372

Unless otherwise indicated, Scripture quotations are taken from the *Holy Bible, New International Version*®. Copyright © 1973, 1978, 1984 by International Bible Society. Used by permission of Zondervan Publishing House. All rights reserved.

Other versions used are

THE MESSAGE—Scripture taken from *THE MESSAGE.* Copyright © by Eugene H. Peterson, 1993, 1994, 1995. Used by permission of NavPress Publishing Group.
NASB—Scripture taken from the NEW AMERICAN STANDARD BIBLE®, Copyright © 1960, 1962, 1963, 1968, 1971, 1973, 1975, 1977, 1995 by The Lockman Foundation. Used by permission.
NLT—Scripture quotations marked (*NLT*) are taken from the *Holy Bible,* New Living Translation, copyright © 1996. Used by permission of Tyndale House Publishers, Inc., Wheaton, Illinois 60189. All rights reserved.

Rights for publishing this book in other languages are contracted by Gospel Light Worldwide, the international nonprofit ministry of Gospel Light. Gospel Light Worldwide also provides publishing and technical assistance to international publishers dedicated to producing Sunday School and Vacation Bible School curricula and books in the languages of the world. For additional information, visit www.gospellightworldwide.org; write to Gospel Light Worldwide, P.O. Box 3875, Ventura, CA 93006; or send an e-mail to info@gospellightworldwide.org.

table of contents

Part One: Surrender

One: Surrender—A Peculiar Calling · · · · · · · · · · · · · · · · · · 9

Two: The Essence of Faith · 17

Three: Time to Say Goodbye—
    Surrendering People and Possessions · · · · · · · · · · · 23

Four: Fishergirls—
    What It Means to Be a Faithful Follower · · · · · · · · · 30

Five: It's All About Trust · 37

Six: Ready, Set, Jump! · 45

Part Two: Forgiveness

Seven: Defining Forgiveness · 53

Eight: Friendship and Forgiveness · · · · · · · · · · · · · · · · · · 59

Nine: Honor and Respect · 65

Ten: Mirror, Mirror, on the Wall . . . · · · · · · · · · · · · · · · · 72

Eleven: Tough Love · 77

Twelve: Forgive Because You Have Been Forgiven · · · · · · 83

one: surrender: a peculiar calling

For whoever wants to save his life will lose it, but whoever loses his life for me will find it.
Matthew 16:25

Have you ever given up? Just thrown in the towel and said, "I quit!" Well, that's exactly what Jesus wants you to do. Okay, not in *everything* you do, but when it comes to running your own life, that's what He wants—for you to surrender *all* to Him. He wants you to hand over the reins, give up control and admit that, on your own, you don't have a fighting chance!

We live in a world in which taking control of our own life (and often trying to control the lives of others) is normal and expected. To drop the big dreams and decisions of our life into the hands of some unseen god sounds crazy to most people, but as God's girls, that is what we do. We believe in the unseen, and we trust that God has the best plan for our lives.

- **According to Matthew 16:25, what does Jesus guarantee to those who surrender their lives to Him?**

RUNNIN'

All right, grab a pen and get the wheels of your imagination turning. If you could do *anything* in the world you wanted to do for a career—no limitations, no exceptions, no "buts"—what would you do?

Maybe you'd be a prima ballerina, a fashion designer, a doctor, a firefighter, or a dog walker—whatever inspires you! Or maybe it's a combination of a few things that you'd love, love, love to spend the rest of your life doing.

- **However crazy (or common) it might sound, write your wildest dream job in the space provided.**

Now imagine that you have this dream job and that you're bringing in lots of cash doing it—*and* that you've just met the man of your dreams. Then one day, for no apparent reason, God tells you to give it all up, sell everything and move to India. Let that sink in for a minute.

- **What would your first thoughts be? How would you respond?**

- **Would you do it?**

Of course, it's not *always* this dramatic—often He asks us to give up some of the little things first so that we can build up our faith and trust Him with the more important ones. But ultimately, God calls each of us to surrender every hope, dream, possession, passion and person in our lives to fully love and serve Him.

As a young teenager, it took a lot of heartache to get me to that point. It took my running from God and my parents and everything that was right to bring me to a place of total surrender. Let me explain. (Here's where we start to get a little bit more open with each other.)

Let's back up a few years. I asked Jesus into my heart one summer when I was 12 (actually, I asked and I asked and I asked many times!). Shortly after, another significant thing began to happen to me: *boys*. Having shed my childhood chub to reveal a svelte new figure, the opposite sex suddenly found me attractive. No longer was I a fat kid to be teased but a girl to be reckoned with! Soon I had my first boyfriend, then my first kiss, then my first heartbreak, then my second boyfriend, then . . . and thus began a sad and increasingly scandalous pattern that carried throughout my teens.

At age 15, sometime during the fall of my sophomore year of high school, I got caught in a massive lie. It wasn't just the lie (or rather, several lies) that was exposed—it was the lie that I was *living* that finally came into the light.

I don't think my parents were ready for my rapid transition from girlhood to girlfriend. I wasn't even supposed to date until I was 16! Oh, but I did! I used my friends and my good-girl image to get what I wanted. I never actually snuck out—rather, I "lied out" until, one night, things went too far.

After lying to my parents about staying the night at a friend's house, I snuck off with my boyfriend (I thought I was so sly). My friend's mom called my mom, my mom called my other friend (who happened not to be in on this one), and she called me and tipped me off that my parents were looking for me (and that I was about to lose her friendship for putting her in the middle of my scheme).

A wild goose chase began. My friends covered for me, my boyfriend lied for me, and I kept running—in another friend's car, all over town—until I finally had to give up. I called my parents from *another* friend's house and tried to negotiate with them *on my terms.* No sir-ee-Bob! They came and dragged me away. Trust broken, image shattered, lies exposed—the shame was almost more than I could bear.

- **Have you ever been caught in a lie?**

- **What did you do when you got caught?**

- **How did you feel about yourself?**

- **Have you ever run from anything in your life (figuratively or literally—this could have been a dog, a bee, a person, a situation, something you knew you needed to do, or something in a dream you had)? Describe that situation in the space provided.**

- **How did the "chase" finally end?**

a severe kindness

The lyrics of a song I love say, "Desire's led me right to the thing that has me runnin' back to you."[1] It's so true! The very thing that had me running to hang on to my own desires ended up bringing me full circle, back to the feet of Jesus—much more humble and broken, however, than if I had done the right thing to begin with.

So the story didn't end there in a heap of snot and tears on my bedroom floor. No, although I camped out there for about three days, too ashamed to show my face to my family and restricted from seeing any friends, I wasn't alone. God met me there in my room that weekend. And He didn't come enraged, reminding me of all the crimes I had committed. Rather, He gently (but powerfully) whispered to my heart, *Why are you running from Me?*

Sometimes a gentle word can break chains, and His word to me really did! It broke all resistance in me. I decided then to give up the fight and give control to Jesus.

- **If you have a Bible handy (and you should), look up Romans 2:4. What does it say about God's kindness?**

One: Surrender—A Peculiar Calling

- In my story, how did God show me kindness?

- How did that lead to my repentance?

- What's your story? How has God demonstrated His kindness (even if it was a severe type of kindness) to you?

raise a WHITE FLAG!

surrender (surrender) v.—to give (oneself) up into the power of another especially as a prisoner; n—the action of yielding one's person or giving up the possession of something especially into the power of another[2]

In battle, the symbol for surrender is a white flag. For centuries, soldiers have used this universal sign to say, "Hey! We give up! You win! Don't kill us!" It signals to the opponent that the one with the white flag is unarmed, willing to give control of the outcome over to the other person, and that he or she is willing to give in to the other's power.

- **Are there any battles raging in your life or in your heart for which you need to raise the white flag?**

- **Another definition of surrender says to "relinquish possession or control of."[3] What do you feel God has called you to give possession or control of to Him?**

Shortly after my white-flag situation, I broke up with my boyfriend and surrendered my heart to God. I also gave up something else that was holding me back from fully following Jesus—my music.

Now, back then (before the days of iPod Nanos and mp3s), we listened to tapes—CDs weren't even around yet. (Do you even know what a cassette tape is? Ha!) And my tapes had some sensual lyrics on them. I'm not saying that all my tapes were all bad, and I'm not saying that listening to secular music is bad. The point here is that I *knew*, without a doubt, that the Holy Spirit was asking me to get rid of any non-Christian music I had.

It was a radical test of my faith. It was more symbolic than anything: reaffirming to myself, to God and to my closest friends that my lifestyle had changed. I remember that day in my room when I passionately ripped all of the tape out of those cassettes, ribbons of my sinful past tumbling into the trash can. Even Whitney Houston was ripped to shreds.

My best friend at the time was appalled. "Why didn't you give those to me?!" she whined. "I love that group!" She didn't quite get the point. Oh well, that's okay; people didn't get Noah when he built the ark either, but he ended up saving the human race by doing it. So I wasn't too worried about her surprise and sarcasm in the face of my sacrifice. I did what I had to do, and God was pleased with me. I felt as if I were starting fresh.

- **Have you ever made a sacrifice for Christ that other people couldn't understand or perhaps thought you were nuts for doing?**

- **Make a list right now of any ungodly thing that you think you might be hanging on to** that really belongs in the dumpster (such as a relationship, music, foul language, magazines, a bad habit). You might even want to evaluate some good things that you think might be taking up too much of your life.

💬 Who would be a good person to talk to about these things (a mentor, youth leader, older friend, sibling or parent)? If possible, call or e-mail that person right now and let him or her know what you want to do. Or, if you're in a group or doing this study with another person, let them know now what those things are and why you need to sacrifice them.

cosmic CONTROL freak or father of FREEDOM?

Surrender seems like a peculiar calling. Why would God have us do it? I mean, why wouldn't He just say, "Do your best and go for it!" Is He a cosmic control freak or something? *No!* God wants us to surrender our lives to Him so that He can give us so much more!

Hebrews 12:1-2 says, "Let us throw off everything that hinders and the sin that so easily entangles, and let us run with perseverance the race marked out for us. Let us fix our eyes on Jesus, the author and perfecter of our faith, who for the joy set before him endured the cross, scorning its shame, and sat down at the right hand of the throne of God."

Jesus gave His life for us so that we could have eternal life with Him. When we give up our lives in order to receive His, He gives us the following:

- Freedom from sin
- True joy and peace
- Hope for a great future in this life and the life to come
- Relationship with the one and only living God
- Healing in our hearts
- Health in our relationships
- Clear vision and direction

And the list goes on and on. Jesus gave up His life—and you can too! And when you do, He'll be with you every step of the way. He wants to be number one in your life because He knows that the competition only wrecks you if it's not submitted to His authority.

Let's pray.

> Father in heaven, I love You. I want everything in my life to reflect You. Is there anything in my life that is offensive to You or that I haven't completely surrendered control of to You? If there is, please show me and help me to give it up. I trust You with my heart. Thank You for loving me and for only wanting what's best for me. In Jesus' name, amen.

Notes

1. "Runnin'," GRITS, *The Art of Translation*, Gotee Records, 2002.
2. Merriam-Webster Online Dictionary, s.v. "surrender." http://www.m-w.com/dictionary (accessed June 6, 2006).
3. Dictionary.com, s.v. "surrender." http://www.dictionary.com (accessed June 6, 2006).

two: THE essence OF faith

> *And without faith it is impossible to please God, because anyone who comes to him must believe that he exists and that he rewards those who earnestly seek him.*
> Hebrews 11:6

Did you know that risk takers impress God? That's right, God delights in courageous people who dare to do what others might think is outrageous. From what I read in the Bible, it appears that God would much rather see us be overly courageous than overly cautious, and that He blesses those who choose to trust Him in the face of the impossible.

💬 Do you consider yourself a risk taker? Why or why not?

Not sure? Take this short quiz to get an idea:

1. When a new student comes into my class or to my youth group I

    (a) am the first to introduce myself
    (b) don't know; I haven't noticed any new people lately
    (c) feel a little shy—I just mind my own business unless we naturally happen to meet

2. Of the following activities, I would most like to

    (a) go rock climbing
    (b) stay in bed and read
    (c) watch movies with the girls

3. Sharing my faith with a complete stranger is

    (a) exciting! I love it!
    (b) something I've never done before
    (c) weird—I feel really awkward doing it

4. If I find an outfit that I totally love but is way different from what most people at my school would wear, I

    (a) buy it! Who cares what everyone else is wearing?
    (b) might get it, but I'd only wear it if I was trying to look funky for something
    (c) leave it on the rack

You're a bold and adventurous soul if you circled mostly or all *a*s. If you circled mostly *b*s and *c*s, I think what's ahead will encourage, inspire and challenge your faith.

GIANTS in the land

Let's talk about two men in the Old Testament who were risk takers. Joshua and Caleb were 2 of 12 spies Moses sent out to check out the land that God had promised to the Israelites. He commissioned them to find out as much as they could about the place and the people. Was the land rich and green, or was it wild and barren? Were the people puny or powerful? Did they live in mansions or makeshift tents?

What the spies found astounded them. The land *was* beautiful—a paradise! *But* it wasn't perfect—there were *giants* in it, people famed for their fierce nature and superhuman stature. It was both a wonderful and a fearsome sight.

After 40 days on the road, the spies returned and gave the following report to Moses and the people of Israel:

> "We went to the land to which you sent us and, oh! It *does* flow with milk and honey! Just look at this fruit! The only thing is that the people who live there are fierce, their cities are huge and well fortified. Worse yet, we saw descendants of the giant Anak. Amalekites are spread out in the Negev; Hittites, Jebusites, and Amorites hold the hill country; and the Canaanites are established on the Mediterranean Sea and along the Jordan."

> *Caleb interrupted, called for silence before Moses and said, "Let's go up and take the land—now. We can do it."*
>
> *But the others said, "We can't attack those people; they're way stronger than we are." They spread scary rumors among the People of Israel. They said, "We scouted out the land from one end to the other—it's a land that swallows people whole. Everybody we saw was huge. Why, we even saw the Nephilim giants. . . . Alongside them we felt like grasshoppers"* (Numbers 13:27-33, THE MESSAGE).

Ten of the spies let what they saw dictate their feelings and then let their feelings determine their faith (or lack of it, I should say). Joshua and Caleb, however, made their feelings submit to their faith. They took what they saw as an opportunity to trust God, and said:

> *The land we walked through and scouted out is a very good land—very good indeed. If GOD is pleased with us, he will lead us into that land, a land that flows, as they say, with milk and honey. And he'll give it to us. Just don't rebel against GOD! And don't be afraid of those people. Why, we'll have them for lunch! They have no protection and GOD is on our side. Don't be afraid of them!* (Numbers 14:7-9, THE MESSAGE).

💬 **Who do you identify with more, the 10 or the 2?**

💬 **Have you ever been in a situation in which there was a battle between your faith and your feelings? Between what your eyes saw and what your heart believed? Which side won?**

In Romans 14:23, Paul states that anything that we do in life that does not come from an attitude of faith is sin. That's right—*sin*. So if we see "giants" in our life—circumstances, relationships, decisions regarding our future—we need to ask Jesus to give us the faith to face them.

We all know the age-old story of David and Goliath. David was a teen, just like you. His brothers were the big warriors; he was merely a shepherd boy. But he was a boy who had faced lions and bears with faith, so when the time came to confront Goliath, he was able to confidently say, "Your servant has killed both the lion and the bear; this uncircumcised Philistine will be like one of them, because he has defied the armies of the living God. The

LORD who delivered me from the paw of the lion and the paw of the bear will deliver me from the hand of this Philistine" (1 Samuel 17:36-37).

Call Me Crazy

I've done some crazy things in my lifetime, mainly in the arena of missions and international travel. It all started when I was a teenager. Just weeks after graduation, I took my first overseas flight—to Albania. Although this small country is located in the Mediterranean region, it wasn't exactly a tourist destination. Only about a year before my trip, Albania was freed from the grip of a communist government. For nearly 50 years, it had experienced little to no religious liberty.

Now it makes me laugh to think that an eclectic mix of on-fire teenagers were some of the first people to reintroduce Albanians to the gospel! At the time, though, I'm sure my parents were not laughing about sending their baby girl to such an unstable place.

- **Have you ever gone anywhere or done anything that seemed totally crazy to others at the time?**

- **How did they react? Did they support or discourage you from doing it?**

I took another cross-cultural leap when, after college, I spent several months alone in Brazil. I had initially gone as a representative of a missions group, but I ended up living in a house full of Brazilians (20, to be exact), none of whom spoke English! It was a difficult season, but I went in faith, believing that I was where God had called me to go, doing what He'd called me to do. I left Brazil a much bolder (and a bilingual) person!

On another trip with the same organization, I led a small team of dancers on a tour through a few towns in India. One night, after sharing my faith with about 1,000 Indians who were watching our show, I got word that a militant Hindu group was somewhere in the crowd, angry with us, stirring up strife.

The next day my picture appeared in their newspaper! I loved the photo they took of me, but the story was, well, not so flattering! Local officials took our passports and threatened to kick us out of the country. We prayed that God would protect us. Not only did we get to stay (unharmed), but in the next town, we saw several hundred people give their lives to Christ! The officials in *that* town even invited our Indian brothers back to share the gospel again!

the prayer of **Faith**

It was on that same trip that a group of guys who were traveling with us preached to and prayed for students at a school for the deaf. The young man preaching (he was only about 20 years old) said, "Who wants prayer to receive hearing?" (Wow, what a bold step of faith!). Twenty children came up to the stage. When my friend said, "In Jesus' name, be healed!" his teammates behind him gave a loud clap. All 20 children turned to see what they had *heard!* All of them received their hearing back that day!

> **Have you ever prayed for someone to be healed of a sickness, disease or other physical problem? If so, what happened? If not, why not?**

James 5:16 reads, "The prayer of a righteous man is powerful and effective." Do you know what that means? *If you are walking with Jesus, your prayers have power!*

Jesus Himself said, "Anyone who has faith in me will do what I have been doing. He will do even greater things than these, because I am going to the Father. And I will do whatever you ask in my name, so that the Son may bring glory to the Father. You may ask me for anything in my name, and I will do it" (John 14:12-14).

But we don't have faith in *faith*. It's not that there's some magic hocus-pocus out there or something that we say or do to manipulate God. We have faith in the Father, in the authority and power that Jesus won for us on the cross, and in the Holy Spirit who fills and enables us to do all the things that Jesus did and more!

getting CREATIVE

Throughout all of my crazy adventures, I kept journals. Not just the kind that you write in—I put pictures, drawings, magazine clippings, quotes, dried flowers and all kinds of stuff in them. With this in mind, here's an activity that will require some attention and a little bit of time but will be lots of fun and as creative as you want it to be—and you can keep it going long after you're finished with this book.

Get a notebook or a journal that's at least 8" X 8" (the bigger the better, and blank, unlined pages are best) or get a big piece of poster board that you can glue things on to. Gather old magazines, a pair of scissors, glue and/or double-sided tape and some colored pencils or pens. Call this your "Faith Journey" journal or collage. Fill it with pictures, quotes, verses, journal entries, drawings and any other nifty things you desire that reflect where you are in your faith walk. Include your doubts and fears and also your goals and the promises God has given you. Let this be a tool of expression and growth for you as you record all that God is teaching you in your journey to your promised land.

Pray with me.

> Lord Jesus, You are the author of my faith. I trust in You completely. Help me when I lack faith—help me be like Joshua and Caleb and David. I want to take risks for Your kingdom, and I want to inspire others to have great faith with me! I'm excited about this journey. I Love You!

three: time to say goodbye—surrendering people and possessions

And everyone who has left houses or brothers or sisters or father or mother or children or fields for my sake will receive a hundred times as much and will inherit eternal life.
Matthew 19:29

PACK RATS

Let's start with stuff. Most people have a lot of it lying around. My parents (who are amazing people, don't get me wrong) are like that. They're pack rats with closets and vacated rooms and a garage full of *stuff*—some of it in use, most of it not.

Oh, I'm guilty of being a bit messy myself. It's not so much that I don't get rid of stuff, but that the stuff I have tends to find its way to the floor and to random piles here and there. Anyone out there relate?

> What does your bedroom look like? Are you a neat-nick or an artsy type with "creative organization" at work in your space?

Whatever your style, here's a project for you. Go into your room and find the most cluttered spot in it. It could be in your closet, under your bed, on your desk, or—for some of you—scattered across the entire floor. Now, get two bags or boxes. Take the next 15 minutes to sort through this pile. Ask yourself, *What do I* really *need and use here?* Put the real garbage in one of the bags or boxes, and put the stuff that you don't use—but that someone else might be able to—in the other, to give away.

If you're a total neat freak (no piles, no mess, no clutter), take this time to sift through your clothes and see whether there's anything there that you can get rid of.

- What did you find in your pile? Was it hard to get rid of anything? Did you sense that God was saying, "Give that away," even though you might still like it and use it?

- Remember how, when I was 15, I got rid of my tapes? Is there anything like that in your life that you believe God is asking you to give up? Take a minute right now to ask Him. Use this space to write down anything that comes to mind.

sacrifices

Who would've thought you could learn spiritual lessons from something as fun as cleaning your room? You sorted through and got rid of things you don't use, but the truth is that sometimes God will call you to let go of things you love and use all the time. He will ask you to surrender even the good things.

Take my friend Nicole, for example. Nicole is a fabulous dancer. (I looked up to her in seventh grade, and I still look up to her!) But there came a season in her life, shortly after she graduated from high school, when God called her to lay down her dancing. It was her passion, but, out of obedience to God, she let it go.

- Why would God ask Nicole to do this? Why would He give her a gift, passion, talent or skill and then ask her to abandon it?

Three: Time to Say Goodbye—Surrendering People and Possessions

💬 **In Matthew 19:29, what does Jesus say will be given to those who leave their possessions and their passions for His sake?**

After Nicole's decision to give up dance indefinitely, God took her on an incredible journey—both spiritually and geographically. Long story short, she ended up spending roughly two years in service with a major missions organization. For nearly half that time, she lived in the country of Ukraine. There, she saw dozens of Ukrainian and Russian students' lives transformed by the gospel, and she had the opportunity to personally disciple several of them.

Would you say Nicole's sacrifice was worth it? Well, it gets better. While leading an outreach to St. Petersburg, Russia, a woman whom she'd never seen before approached her in a church. This Russian babushka (as the older women are called) had been watching Nicole try the Israeli dancing that the Russian women were doing. The babushka came up to her, speaking rapidly in Russian. Although Nicole had no clue what the woman was saying, her heart was gripped by it. She turned to the translator, who then interpreted what the babushka had said: "You were created to dance. You must dance before the Lord. That is what He has called you to do!"

Nicole fell to her knees and wept. God was going to restore her passion back to her! And He did. Since that wonderful day, Nicole has earned her degree in modern dance and has taught and performed professionally for years. Whatever she gave up to God during that season, He would restore to her—and more—in the years ahead. She honored Him, and He in turn honored her for her obedience.

💬 **Has God ever asked you to give up a significant passion or possession?**

💬 **If so, what was your response?**

💬 **Why do you think He did that?**

💬 **What have been the results so far?**

if you **love** somebody ...

There's an old saying (and a song by Sting) that says, "If you love somebody, set them free." Jesus has His own version of this philosophy. Let's look at the book of Matthew.

In Matthew 10:37, Jesus says, "Anyone who loves his father or mother more than me is not worthy of me; anyone who loves his son or daughter more than me is not worthy of me." In other words, Jesus was saying, "If you love *Me*, set *them* free." *You have to be willing to love Jesus more than you love even your own mom or dad!*

Luke 14:26 takes it a step further: "If anyone comes to me and does not hate his father and mother, his wife and children, his brothers and sisters—yes, even his own life—he cannot be my disciple."

Whoa! That seems a little over the top!

THE MESSAGE version paraphrases it: "Anyone who comes to me but refuses to let go of father, mother, spouse, children, brothers, sisters—yes, even one's own self!—can't be my disciple."

So, we see how consuming the love of God is. He wants us to trust Him enough to let go of possessions, passions and people—even the good ones—in order to do His will. That doesn't mean that we "hate" our family and friends in the way that we understand the word, but that we are willing to do anything—even leave our dearest loved ones—if God called us to. It also means that we desire to please God more than any human being.

A great example of this kind of sacrificial love is found in the story of Abraham and Isaac. Read the following passage:

> *After all this, God tested Abraham. God said, "Abraham!"*
>
> *"Yes?" answered Abraham. "I'm listening."*
>
> *He said, "Take your dear son Isaac whom you love and go to the land of Moriah. Sacrifice him there as a burnt offering on one of the mountains that I'll point out to you."*
>
> *Abraham got up early in the morning and saddled his donkey. He took two of his young servants and his son Isaac. He had split wood for the burnt offering. He set out for the place God had directed him. On the third day he looked up and saw the place in the*

> distance. Abraham told his two young servants, "Stay here with the donkey. The boy and I are going over there to worship; then we'll come back to you."
>
> Abraham took the wood for the burnt offering and gave it to Isaac his son to carry. He carried the flint and the knife. The two of them went off together.
>
> Isaac said to Abraham his father, "Father?"
>
> "Yes, my son."
>
> "We have flint and wood, but where's the sheep for the burnt offering?"
>
> Abraham said, "Son, God will see to it that there's a sheep for the burnt offering." And they kept on walking together.
>
> They arrived at the place to which God had directed him. Abraham built an altar. He laid out the wood. Then he tied up Isaac and laid him on the wood. Abraham reached out and took the knife to kill his son.
>
> Just then an angel of GOD called to him out of Heaven, "Abraham! Abraham!"
>
> "Yes, I'm listening."
>
> "Don't lay a hand on that boy! Don't touch him! Now I know how fearlessly you fear God; you didn't hesitate to place your son, your dear son, on the altar for me" **(Genesis 22:1-12, THE MESSAGE).**

Can you get any more dramatic than that?! I don't know about you, but I couldn't even imagine tying up a child of mine and putting a knife to his or her throat. I would wonder if I'd been listening to the devil instead of to God!

- **What do you think Abraham was thinking as he walked up the hill to sacrifice his son?**

- **Why was God testing Abraham? What did He say to Abraham in the end?**

- **Are there any relationships that God has called you to put on the altar of sacrifice?**

letting go of love

Of course, God ultimately did not want Abraham to kill Isaac. God values relationships (and *life*) and wants us not only to be at peace with others but to love them deeply as well. There are times, however, when relationships become unhealthy and to sacrifice them is the most loving thing we can do.

Boyfriends. I had way too many of them when I was your age. Please don't follow my example. Yes, I became honest and on fire for Christ after my transformational experience, but even then I had a hard time shaking off boys.

I have to say, too, that if I'd had a mentor in my life, I think things would have been different. So—I know I'm going on a tangent here, but this is huge—find a woman with whom you can be gut-wrenchingly honest and who will give you solid biblical counsel. This could be someone in college, your mom, or even a 70-year-old widow at your church. Of course, first and foremost you want to bring everything to God and to get His take on things. But having a godly mentor in your life is also important for growing up spiritually and emotionally.

Okay, back to boys. After my surrender experience, I stayed away from boys for a little while, but then I started having boyfriends again. I wasn't being promiscuous with them, but in my heart, I knew I shouldn't have been with them at all. They were hindering me from having pure, undistracted devotion to Christ.

- **What does 1 Corinthians 7:32-35 say about this?**

- **This passage speaks of marriage, but how do you think boyfriends might distract you from growing strong in Christ?**

Whether or not you are allowed to date (or want to) at this point in your life, there is one non-negotiable command: Don't date unbelievers (see 2 Corinthians 6:14). God's girls aren't called to be "missionary daters"! Believe me, you won't change them, but they *will* drag you down.

Three: Time to Say Goodbye—Surrendering People and Possessions

My personal take on all of this? Enjoy your friends—guys and girls—and trust God to bring you into a relationship with the right man at the right time. Let purity be your quest, and let Jesus be your first love. Too many young women get tripped up trying to impress guys at too young of an age. Be free of all that! A girl who's confident, friendly and pure is far more attractive anyway than one who's searching for her significance in a boy.

Friends can also hinder and distract you. Even as an adult, I've had to let friendships go because they were a negative influence or because the relationships were with people claiming to know Christ yet living a life that did not reflect Him.

When it was time for me to let go of one particular friendship, I tried to handle the situation graciously. In love and with gentleness, I brought to light a sinful situation that my friend was in. She responded with anger. She did not want me prying into her life (even though at one time we declared ourselves "best friends forever"!). I'm telling you, that's what best friends do—we pry. And we *pray*. We seek the best for one another.

- What do the following verses have to say about this?

    Proverbs 12:15

    Proverbs 27:5-6

    Proverbs 27:17

Anyhow, I actually didn't want to lose this person's friendship, but she was too angry to continue with mine and too enamored with her sin to change.

But does this mean that we are to go around dumping all of our angry, sinful friends? Of course the answer is no. Jesus showed mercy and gave forgiveness, and so should we. The point is that we must be willing to lay our reputations and our relationships down and be willing to be uncool in order to walk as Jesus did. Many people took offense at Him, and many walked away. It was their choice. As for Jesus, He was set on who He was and what God had called Him to do—no apologies. As His friend, He will give you the courage to do as He did.

> Lord Jesus, give me the courage to surrender all to You. Show me what I need to rid my life of. I desire to draw all of my value and self-worth from You—not from boys, friends or anyone else. It is an awesome privilege to serve You! I trust You with every part of my life—every person, every possession and every passion. Amen.

four: fishergirls— what it means to be a faithful follower

"Come, follow me," Jesus said, "and I will make you fishers of men."
Matthew 4:19

Follow (fol low) v. – 1. to go, proceed, or come after ⟨followed the guide⟩; 2. (a) to engage in as a calling or way of life. (b) to walk or proceed along ⟨follow a path⟩; 3. (a) to be or act in accordance with ⟨follow directions⟩. (b) to accept as authority[1]

Which of the three definitions given above for the word "follow" do you think applies to you and your relationship with Jesus?

(a) Definition 1: to go, proceed, or come after
(b) Definition 2: to engage in as a calling or way of life
(c) Definition 3: to be or act in accordance with; to accept as authority
(d) All of the above

You got it; it's (d)! That's right, as believers we follow *after* Jesus—He is our guide, and we follow wherever His Spirit leads us. We also follow Him in such a way that it becomes more than just a religious act—it becomes our *way of life* or our *calling*. Finally, we *act in accordance with* Christ and His Word. We accept His *authority*.

Those are the definitions, but what does it all mean? How do we faithfully follow Christ throughout our lives and help others do the same?

LORDSHIP

Jesus said to the people, "Why do you call me, 'Lord, Lord,' and do not do what I say?" (Luke 6:46). Thus, first and foremost in following Jesus, we must make Him the Lord of our life. That means that we are fully surrendered to Him (remember the definition of that word?) and allow Him total control of our life. We do what He says to do and we avoid the things He says not to do (in other words, sin). But it's also so much more than that! Only Jesus offers us true freedom. Only in Him can we experience true life and true love for all eternity!

- **Have you made the decision to give yourself completely to Jesus and to let Him mold and shape your life as He desires?**

- **If you haven't done that yet and you're ready to surrender to Him now, ask someone who has made that decision to pray with you (someone who's doing this study with you would be a good choice). Take a minute and just talk to God. Tell Him that you believe in Jesus, His Son, and that He died and rose again to bring you life. Ask Him to fill you with that life right now.**

- **If you're already walking with Christ, list three people whom you'd like to lead to Christ:**

    1.

    2.

    3.

- **Now commit to pray for these people daily and see how God moves in their hearts!**

Soul Sister: Trust

180

"Repentance" is a key word in Christianity. One of my favorite Bible studies defines it this way: "True Repentance involves confession of sin, turning *away* from sin and turning *to* God."[2] Repentance is a genuine heart change.

Think of skateboarding. There's a trick called a 180, where a skater is going one way and then, without stopping, flips his board in the opposite direction and starts going back the way he or she came. This is a good image for repentance. You stop going your own way, turn your face toward Jesus and skate as fast as you can toward Him, leaving the past behind.

You might have heard it said that Jesus is either Lord of all or not Lord at all. Cliché though it might be, it's true! And it's to our benefit to leave nothing in our lives outside of God's authority and protection, outside the lordship of Jesus Christ.

- **Are there any areas of unconfessed sin in your life or any struggle that you can't seem to get free from? List some of those issues below. Now, take those issues to God and ask Him for forgiveness, freedom and for help to change.**

Mark 1:4 says, "And so John came, baptizing in the desert region and preaching a baptism of repentance for the forgiveness of sins." God wants to forgive us and give us a new start!

- **We should also share what's going on in our lives (even the deepest, darkest parts) with other trusted believers. What does James 5:16 say about this?**

THE GREATEST COMMANDMENT

Okay, so you love God more than life. Now what?

Four: Fishergirls—What It Means to Be A Faithful Follower

💬 **In Matthew 22:37-38, Jesus said that loving God with all of your heart, soul and mind is the greatest commandment of all. What did He say is the second greatest commandment (v. 39)?**

As God's girl, you are an ambassador of His love. You get to *shine* the amazing love of Christ to everyone you meet! This includes your family, friends, fellow students and perfect strangers.

Because God is love (see 1 John 4:8,16) and you are God's daughter, you can love others as He does! That kind of love is pure, unselfish, generous and truthful. Take a look at the following chart. In what ways do you best show love? Where could you make some improvements? Mark each characteristic accordingly.

I am . . .	Doing great!	Pretty good	Don't even ask me this one!
Patient			
Kind			
Not jealous			
Humble			
Polite			
Unselfish			
Not easily irritated			
Not one to hold grudges			
Full of faith			
Full of hope			
Unfailing in my love for others			

Check out 1 Corinthians 13 to get a better grip on this one. You know, sometimes it's the people we actually love the most, or who are closest to us, who are the hardest to love. That was my challenge as a teenager—to really love my parents, brother and sister 1 Corinthians 13 style. So start closest to your heart—practice lovin' on the peeps closest to you!

spreadin' the LOVE

Part of being a truly loving person, and therefore a faithful follower of Christ, is to be one who spreads the love. We gotta share the message!

Maybe you've heard it called the Great Commission or evangelism. Hmm . . . might sound a little intimidating, but, you know, God has used many young people throughout the ages to spread the good news and accomplish His purposes. You are in a very cool place right now as far as your witness for Christ is concerned! As a teenager, you have mad potential to influence your world.

True love speaks the truth. True love takes others with it. True love wants anyone and everyone to meet Jesus and to see their lives transformed by Him. While there's no set formula for doing this, one of the best and most effective ways is simply to share Christ through your friendship with others and through your lifestyle. Pray for people that God puts in your path and look for the opportunity to share Christ with them. Then, when given an opportunity, *speak*!

Although witnessing one to one is great, sometimes sharing the gospel with larger groups is a good way to go. What are some ways that you can take Christ to your community? Many people won't go with you to church, but they will go to an event that interests them.

Take my friends May and Louie, for example. Hip-hop culture is huge in Seattle, and the underground break-dance scene is rising in popularity. So my two friends took the initiative to rally a bunch of us together to plan a battle (a break-dance competition). Months of prayer and preparation went into the event. My friends recruited famed break-dancers as judges and DJs from a couple of well-known Christian hip-hop groups. They rented an old community center (with lots of charm and character) in the heart of Seattle's International District. They offered a $1,000 prize to the best team of two.

More than 350 people heard the gospel that night. It was sandwiched between a mix of DJs and dancers, competition and community. And the battle went on—both in the natural and the spiritual. The 20-plus people who responded to the message are now getting plugged into local churches and/or attending an urban Bible study started by my innovative friends.

The point of this story? *A faithful follower of Christ takes the gospel out of the box and into the community!*

Four: Fishergirls—What It Means to Be A Faithful Follower

- Use the space below to brainstorm ideas for reaching your friends and your generation. This could include having bubble tea with a non-Christian friend, or it might be something bigger and bolder (I have one friend who uses magic—illusions, to clarify—to preach the gospel!). The sky's the limit!

FAITH

Another huge element of being a faithful follower is in the word itself—"faith"! Don't leave home without it! And God gives it to everyone who loves Him (check out Romans 12:3).

Faith sees Jesus rather than the obstacles in front of it. Faith chooses to do what's right, even when what's wrong feels like the better option. Faith holds on when all hope seems lost. Faith believes that no matter what the circumstances, God will see you through. Faith *trusts* God in all things and at all times (we'll get to that in the next session).

a divine romance

Finally, faithful followers of Christ recognize that they are in a divine romance with Jesus. Actually, this is really the foundation of becoming a follower. The Lord first wins our hearts to His. He is the One who is unfailingly faithful, the One who loves us with love beyond our understanding.

Do you know how passionately loved you are by God the Father? He calls you the Bride of Christ. Think of a man on his wedding day getting ready to watch the love of his life walk down the aisle (girls aren't the only ones who get giddy you know!). Ask your father or a faithful man of God how he felt when he saw his bride walking toward him on their wedding day. That is the way God feels about *you*!

- Take a few minutes to write a love letter. You can write it here or in your Faith Journey journal. Write it to Jesus. Tell Him how much you love Him and want to know His love.

Pray with me or use your love letter as a prayer to God.

> Jesus, I so long to follow You faithfully. I love You. I am desperate for You! Please be the Lord of everything in my life. Show me if there's any sin in my heart and help me to change. Holy Spirit, I need You to give me power to love people and to share Jesus with them. Increase my faith! Help me to really get Your love for me and to be transformed by it. I'm stoked to be Your Bride! Amen.

Notes

1. Merriam-Webster Online Dictionary, s.v. "follow." http://www.webster.com (accessed June 6, 2006).
2. Rice Broocks, Phil Bonasso and Steve Murrell, *Biblical Foundations* (Brentwood, TN: Every Nation Productions, 1998), n.p.

five: it's all about trust

Trust God from the bottom of your heart; don't try to figure out everything on your own. Listen for God's voice in everything you do, everywhere you go; he's the one who will keep you on track.
Proverbs 3:5-6, THE MESSAGE

Trust God *from the bottom of your heart*—that's what this verse says. With *all* your heart! Trust such as this knows that the One in whom you trust is good and does everything for your good. That doesn't mean it will always feel good or look good, but, in the end, the Bible says that God works out all things for the good of those who love Him (see Romans 8:28).

BROKEN TRUST

Hurt happens in life. That's just how it is in a fallen world. People let us down. Parents wound us. Friends disappoint us. We even emotionally injure ourselves at times.

Often when trust is broken, the tendency is to lick our wounds and shrink away, vowing never to go back to that place or trust that person again. But Jesus speaks of forgiveness and of trust restored.

💬 **Have you ever broken anyone's trust? What did you do?**

💬 **What was the final outcome of the situation?**

Soul Sister: Trust

I feel a collage moment coming on . . . grab that journal of yours and create a picture, a poem or something with mixed media (you can even choreograph a dance or write a song if that's your thing!) that tells a story about your trust being broken. Think of a specific incident or relationship and express it creatively. After you do that, answer the following question:

- **What was the main image or word (or movement) that you used to describe the pain of your trust being broken? Why did you choose that image, word or movement?**

THE ULTIMATE BETRAYAL

Visualize something with me. Imagine yourself in a shady garden. Daylight has turned to dusk, and as it grows darker, the *feeling* of the place grows darker as well. You're with a few of your trusted friends, yet you feel totally alone. Your throat tightens. Your heart races. You feel a thousand pounds of weight on your shoulders—stress like you've never felt before.

Your friends hang back, but you decide to go further into the garden to pray. Sweat beads up on your forehead and on your whole body, sending a chill across your skin. It's as though you hear whispers in the darkness, tormenting you, accusing you, threatening you. You turn back to find your friends, but in your moment of need, they have all abandoned you. Even worse, you suddenly realize that one of them is standing behind you—with a knife to your back.

Is this a scene out of a horror flick or something?! No! It's a picture I wanted to paint to give you a sense (a very imperfect, miniscule taste) of what the ultimate betrayal of trust might have been like. It happened more than 2,000 years ago in a garden called Gethsemane.

Go with me to Mark 14:32-50.

- **How do verses 33 and 34 describe what Jesus was feeling in that hour?**

- **What did Jesus ask the Father in verses 35 and 36?**

Five: It's All About Trust

- What did His disciples do in His hour of need?

- How did Judas act when he betrayed Jesus?

- Focus on verse 50. What did Jesus' most trusted friends do when His enemies came for Him?

TRUST Restored

As you know—and as was the will of God—men arrested, abused and nailed Jesus to a cross. All the while, Peter, one of His nearest and dearest, stood back at a distance, denying that he even knew Jesus.

But Jesus' story doesn't end there. He rose from the dead! (All our girlhood fairy tales have at least one thing in common with the Truth: a happy ending!) Everything that He went through—His dying, His resurrection and His return to the Father—happened for a reason, a reason called restoration, or reconciliation. He took our punishment and our pain to the cross with Him in order to pay for our sins and to restore us to a right relationship with God. Where trust and relationship had been broken, Jesus brought reconciliation.

This is true for all of us and for all people throughout history who will receive it. It was also true for one very close friend of Jesus.

Read John 21:15-19.

Soul Sister: Trust

> **Does Jesus sound angry with Peter in this passage? Does He bring up Peter's past?**

> **What can we learn from Jesus' attitude toward Peter?**

Notice that Jesus repeats to Peter two of the first key words He ever spoke to him: "Follow Me!" It fascinates me that Peter, who totally broke trust with Jesus a few days before, is now entrusted with caring for the entire new Church! Jesus Himself restored their relationship (even though He was the one who was hurt by Peter) and restored Peter to a place of honor and trust. (We'll look at this amazing kind of forgiveness in the next session.)

TRUSTWORTHINESS

That brings up a good point: being trustworthy. Are you ready to be entrusted with the great things of God? Do you trust Him to do great things in your life? Take the following short quiz.

1. **When given a great opportunity, I usually**

   (a) wonder what to do with it
   (b) feel totally inadequate to do it
   (c) run with it!

2. **If I were to be given an unexpected chunk of money, I would**

   (a) wonder what to do with it
   (b) go on a shopping spree
   (c) pray and ask God what to do with it

3. **When my clothes come out of the dryer, I usually**

   (a) throw them on top of the growing pile of wrinkled clothes in my closet (who cares, I'll iron them when I need them, right?)
   (b) hang them up or fold them and put them away
   (c) what do you mean what do I do with them? My mom takes care of that!

4. When I think I'm talented in something or would like to try a new sport or activity, I usually

    (a) practice and try to get more involved in whatever it is
    (b) really want to try it, but I feel scared—there are so many other people who are better at it than I am
    (c) forget about it—I wouldn't really be all that good at it anyway

When God gives us a gift, He expects us to use it! In Matthew 25:14-28, Jesus tells a parable about a master who entrusted three servants with money. Two of the servants used the money to double what their master had given them. The third, however, felt scared, so he did nothing with it—he actually buried it in the ground and hid it! He was afraid he'd lose it and get in trouble.

- That doesn't sound unreasonable, does it? However, in the parable, the master became furious with this third servant. Why do you think the master got so angry with him?

- What does this tell us about God's character and what He wants us to do with the gifts and responsibilities He gives to us?

You know, the world gives us a lot of reasons to feel insecure about ourselves, telling us we're not skinny enough, not smart enough, not stylish enough to do this or that without such and such a product. Look in any fashion magazine and you will see that this is the case. But God tells us that we *are* good enough in Christ. He says we are more than conquerors (see Romans 8:37), and He wants us to have the attitude of a conqueror.

So what does this have to do with being trustworthy? Everything! Whether it's your clothing or your musical ability or the people whom God has placed in your life, God wants you to treat each and every thing and person in your life with respect and confidence. His Word says to do everything that you do to the glory of Christ (see 1 Corinthians 10:31 and Colossians 3:23).

- List a few of your talents or abilities.

- List a few special material items you own (such as clothing, an iPod, a computer, a guitar, or a special bank account you have).

- Now list a few special people in your life.

Looking at these lists, consider how trustworthy you've been with each thing or person. Next to each one, jot down a little note saying how you could better cultivate that gift, care for that thing, or encourage that person.

RADICAL TRUST

Faith and trust go hand in hand. It takes faith to step out and do great things for God. It takes trust to surrender your greatest dreams, desires and possessions to Him.

- Look back at that list of your talents and abilities. What if God asked you to give up the thing you're most gifted at (remember my friend Nicole)? It could be dance, soccer, academics. What would you do? How would you feel if you knew in your heart that you needed to let that thing go and didn't know if you would ever get to do it again?

- Why would God give us a gift and ask us to sacrifice it? (Think of the story of Abraham and Isaac.)

Sometimes, God tests our heart to make sure that there's no idolatry in it (in other words, to make sure that we don't love something or somebody more than we love Him) and to see whether we trust Him. In Malachi 3:10, God told the Israelites to bring their tithes to Him, and then promised to bless them if they did, saying, "Test me in this . . . and see if I will not throw open the floodgates of heaven and pour out so much blessing that you will not have room enough for it."

The same is true for you and me! We are to trust God with our money by giving Him (giving to your church) at least 10 percent of whatever we earn. You earn $10, you give Him $1 (or more!). You earn $250, you give Him $25. It's that simple.

You can apply this principle to *everything* in your life, because it's all a gift from God anyway! Your talents, your time, your money—commit it all to Him. Trust Him and see whether He won't do marvelous things with whatever you give Him. So be like the stewards in the parable who trusted their master and dared to do great things with what he had given them. Don't be like the one who was afraid, hid his talents and ended up losing everything.

like butterflies

Our dreams can sometimes be like butterflies. We try to capture them, but they fly away from us. And if we do catch them, it's hard to let them go.

Imagine that you are in a field and that you've got a net filled with beautiful and brightly colored butterflies that you've just caught. Now imagine Jesus telling you to release them to Him. He does this with our dreams and hopes, asking us to trust Him with them. If they're truly

His dreams for us, He'll return them to us, bigger, brighter and more beautiful than they ever were before.

One big dream that lots of girls have is to meet and marry their Prince Charming. I know it was (and still is!) one of mine. But I held that dream a little too tightly for most of my life and, like a fragile butterfly in my hand, I crushed it with wrong relationships. I tried so hard to make each boyfriend fit the mold of who I thought my husband should be (poor guys!).

Finally, after much suffering in this area, I surrendered this desire to God and chose to trust Him—no matter how long it took (if ever). As I write, my "happily ever after" hasn't yet happened. Do I still hope and have faith that it will? Yes! Am I worried and trying to make it happen myself? Nope! Until that time comes, I am like a Sleeping Beauty, resting in God and His great wisdom for my life.

- Take a minute to write about some of your heart's deepest dreams. You can use the space here or use your personal journal. If you feel that you are ready, write a prayer to God, surrendering those dreams to Him. Let Him know that you trust Him with your life and that you want to give it all to Him.

> *Jesus, I want to release my hopes and dreams to You, but sometimes it's just so hard to let go. Give me the strength to trust in You completely and follow the path that You have laid out for my life. Help me to boldly release my gifts, talents and abilities to You so that You can use them for Your glory. I release all that I have to You—it's all Yours anyway! Thank You, Lord. Amen.*

six: ready, set, jump!

Therefore, since we are surrounded by such a great cloud of witnesses, let us throw off everything that hinders and the sin that so easily entangles, and let us run with perseverance the race marked out for us.
Hebrews 12:1

Sometimes, it takes a lot of courage to surrender. Do you remember Smeagol/Gollum in *The Lord of the Rings*? In *The Return of the King,* his refusal to let go of the ring led to his ultimate demise. He had become enslaved by the ring's power—actually, his own desire to possess its power enslaved him. The same thing nearly happened to Frodo as well. In fact, Frodo lost his finger because he could not let go of the ring!

- **What does 2 Peter 2:19 have to say about becoming attached to the things of this world?**

Many of us have prized possessions—music, clothes, boyfriends—that we have a hard time letting go of when we know we're not supposed to be holding on anymore. But hanging on, as Hebrews 12:1 says, *hinders* and *entangles* us. We're not just talking about blatant sin here; we're talking about everything that hinders us from a fruitful, fulfilling walk with God.

- **What does Paul say in 1 Corinthians 6:12 about things that might weaken his faith?**

- **What specifically might be hindering you from growing in your walk with Christ? Do you think you have any "sacred rings" that are so powerful you can hardly detach yourself from them?**

💬 **What's the first step you will take to throw off these things?**

THE **FEAR** FACTOR

Second Timothy 1:7 says, "For God has not given us a spirit of timidity, but a spirit of power, of love and of self-discipline." Girl, you are *bold*! You are strong in Jesus! Romans 8:37 puts it another way, telling us that we overwhelmingly conquer through Christ. Reflect on these verses when you feel fearful about surrendering yourself (or anything else) to God.

Have you ever gone bungee jumping? Not me! No thanks! Falling from great heights does not interest me one bit. But I did drive past one of the original bungee jumping sites when I was traveling through Queenstown, New Zealand (just the sight of it made my stomach lurch!). I have a friend who has done this jump many times. She said it was so hard, each time, to shove herself off the edge of that platform, but that the rush she experienced at the end of the jump was beyond description. She couldn't stop laughing! It gave her energy that lasted for days.

As with life, it's that first step that usually takes the most courage. Even though you know that something has got a hold of you (be it a bungee cord or God), you know there will be a moment (or a season) of free-falling—a time when you're so totally out of control that you can do nothing to stop yourself.

As you grow in faith, often that sensation of free-falling will last longer and longer, because God knows you can handle it, and because you've grown to trust Him. I can say that's been the case in my life. God has so stretched my faith that at times I've felt as though I should have hit bottom, yet He keeps stretching me! And I continue to surrender to Him.

💬 **What are you most afraid of surrendering to God?**

Six: Ready, Set, Jump!

DANDELIONS

Some of you might be very young; others might be about to graduate from high school. Whatever your age or stage in life, you are never too young (or too old!) to surrender your future to God. And, hey—NEWS FLASH—He's already got a plan for it anyway!

💬 **What does Jeremiah 29:11 have to say about your future and God's plans for it?**

Do you know what dandelions look like after they blossom? They turn into a "seed head"—it looks like they have a white cottonlike ball on top of the stem. I used to make wishes and try to blow all the white fluffy seeds off them. If I blew them all off in one breath, I got my wish!

Imagine your dreams and hopes are like those tiny white seeds. Right now, they're all in your head, like the cotton puffs on the dandelion. But when you pray and blow them into God's hands, He is able to take them (and you with them!) to places you have never imagined!

It might seem that what you surrender to God gets scattered in every direction, and maybe you won't see any evidence of those surrendered things for a while, but God takes those seeds and does something miraculous with them. When you choose to trust Him completely, He is able to do far more than you could ever ask for or dream of (see Ephesians 3:20)!

💬 **Grab your journal and write your dreams in it. After you do that, go through your list and one by one pray over each item and release it to God. It might be a good idea to pray your dreams through with a friend or a mentor so that you can encourage each other and remind each other of your courage to surrender everything to God.**

so secure

Where else in the world could be more secure than in the arms of the Father? Maybe your relationship with your own dad didn't reflect this security. Maybe you don't even have a relationship with your father. But there is a Father whom you can trust and in whose arms you can be totally yourself and feel totally safe. Think of a little girl climbing onto her daddy's lap, cuddling there, his big arms around her. That kind of security draws us to surrender all to the Lord. It becomes not a "have to" but a "want to" kind of thing.

I remember nights in Brazil when I was on an outreach in the tropical northeastern part of the country. After most people had gone to bed or were socializing in the dining hall (we were staying at a camp), I would wander across the field to the pool. I'd sit on the steps near the pool, watching the white clouds drift past and letting the breeze brush the day's heat off my skin. God would speak to me there. We'd share such sweet times that I never wanted to leave. Stars would come out as the night grew darker, and I would lie back and share my dreams with God.

I remember one special night—a night when I felt very, very close to Him—a shooting star streaked across the sky. It was breathtaking! I think I cried. As I slowly walked back to my cabin, I said, "Lord, if You heard me tonight, and if that was You that I heard, please show me one more shooting star before I go to bed."

I kept turning around as I walked, looking up, waiting for that star. I got closer to the cabin, and even that seemingly silly wish I surrendered. "Lord," I said, "even if I don't see another star, I believe that I encountered You tonight and that You have good plans for me. I don't doubt You." I stepped in the door and turned around for one last look. As I did, I saw it: a brilliant star burning through the black night.

Needless to say, I slept well that night, secure—and dazzled—in the God I had encountered. His love is the sweetest love, sweeter and more powerful than any father's or friend's or boyfriend's. We can be secure—and we can be amazed—as we surrender all to Him.

GIRLS' NIGHT!

It's time for a girls' night *in*! Gather the girls from your Soul Sister group and/or a few other friends (you'll need at least five people). Get some girls to bring drinks and snacks and others to help you plan the following activities that will help you demonstrate your trust in God and build trust in each other. You can keep this to an evening or have an overnighter. Regardless of which you choose, bring your journals and share some of your creativity and your stories with each other. Cap off the night with prayer and with each girl receiving a word of encouragement.

Take the Plunge!

Alright, this is the next best thing you can do to bungee jumping. First, check with your mom to make sure you have permission to stand on the furniture. Next, have one girl stand on the couch, facing the back of the couch, with her feet close to the edge. Now have two to four girls stand on the ground beneath her and make a "basket" with their arms. Have one girl there as her spotter, standing at the end of the basket so that she's facing the same direction as the girl on the couch. (Put pillows on the ground beneath her—just in case!) Have the girl on the couch cross her arms in front of her and let herself fall back as the girls beneath her keep their arms linked together to catch her. The girl falling back will have to *trust* that her friends beneath will catch her!

Blind Trust

Divide into pairs (if you have an odd number, have a group of three). Place a blindfold on one person in each pair. The one blindfolded will be the follower; the other girl will be the leader. Practice trust (and being trustworthy!) by having the leader lead the follower around the house, the mall, the park, the neighborhood (if it's daylight outside), or wherever else for a few minutes. After a while, have the leader and follower exchange places. Note that the leader can do more than just walk her follower—she can put clothes on her, feed her, lead her around various obstacles using her voice to tell her follower exactly what to do. But remember, this is a *trust* exercise, so be kind to your follower (and remember that you'll be following next!).

Unwind

The following activity will help you remember the verse we began this chapter with, Hebrews 12:1. Have two girls volunteer to stand in the center of your group. Using toilet paper, clothing, tape, yarn, jewelry, hair accessories—whatever you can think of—entangle the girls in the center with stuff (make sure they can breathe!). Take five minutes to do this. At the end of the five minutes, have each girl throw off everything they have been entangled with. The first one to become free of everything wins! Music will make this activity more fun, and a nice prize for the winner will make it more exciting. Take turns being the girls in the center until each girl has had a chance to be the Hebrews 12:1 girl.

After these activities, take a moment to sit down and talk about each activity and how it made you think about trust and surrender. Then grab some ice cream and a good chick flick and have fun!

Pray with me.

> Lord, thank You for showing me that I can trust You. I ask You for the courage to surrender my life and everything in it to You every day! You are my Father; I am secure in You. My hopes, dreams and future are totally secure in You. Thank You for the freedom that true surrender brings. I want to live each day in that freedom and to help others find it too. Please keep showing me how to do that. I Love You! Amen.

PART TWO: Forgiveness

seven: defining forgiveness

This is my blood of the covenant, which is poured out . . . for the forgiveness of sins.
Matthew 26:28

*All the prophets testify about him that everyone who believes in him
receives forgiveness of sins through his name.*
Acts 10:43

*I write to you, dear children, because your sins
have been forgiven on account of his name.*
1 John 2:12

Forgiveness is too great of a subject to start this session with only one verse! It's also a subject too powerful to begin to explain without prayer.

> Lord, will You please meet us here right now and shed light on this topic called forgiveness? Please help us understand what it means to be forgiven, how we get forgiven, how to forgive others and—most of all—how much You love us and what You sacrificed to bring us into a relationship of forgiveness with You. Amen.

THE ESSENCE OF FORGIVENESS

What does it mean to forgive someone? I wasn't really satisfied with the definitions I found in *Webster's Dictionary*, so I'm going to explain it in my words here. "Forgiveness" means that when someone hurts or offends us, we don't hold it against them. It doesn't mean that we pretend a bad thing never happened or that we don't expect the offender to take responsibility for what he or she did, but rather that we don't pay the offender back for it and don't stay mad or offended at him or her. As 1 Peter 4:8 says, "Love covers a multitude of sins."

Love is the essence of forgiveness—it is at its core. Without love, true forgiveness is impossible. Look at it this way: God is love and the source of forgiveness. When we follow His example, we are able to forgive others because He forgave us.

> 💬 **In Matthew 18:21-35, Jesus tells the Parable of the Unforgiving Servant. What does this parable say about forgiveness?**

In this parable, the first servant owed the king millions of dollars—such an amount that it could have only been repaid by selling himself and his whole family into slavery. But the king showed that man mercy (a word we'll get to later) and freed him from *all* debt. He didn't just lower his debt or give him extra time to pay it off, he *erased it all*! The servant no longer owed the king *anything*.

What did that servant do then? He went out and demanded from another servant a few dollars that person owed him! Not only did he not cancel the other guy's debt, but he also had the other servant imprisoned until he could pay back every single cent! He did not know the essence of forgiveness.

We all are like each of these debtors. Some of us have sinned a lot and some a little, but "all have sinned and fall short of the glory of God" (Romans 3:23). Therefore, all of us are in need of forgiveness. We can't bring our sin to heaven with us, so we have to repent (remember session 4?) and receive God's forgiveness.

God's forgiveness is the ultimate. When we accept Jesus as our Savior and Lord, He forgives us of all our sins for all times! He makes us as though we had never sinned at all. He sees us as He sees Christ, clothed in complete holiness and purity.

The power of blood

We can't earn our own forgiveness. Somebody had to earn it for us. Someone had to do something to free us from sin's grip and from the righteous anger of God that burned against us for our sins. That person was Jesus, and He sacrificed His life for us. He bled—let whips and thorns and nails slice through His flesh—to bring us forgiveness.

💬 **What do the following verses communicate about the power of blood?**

According to the Law, one may almost say, all things are cleansed with blood, and without shedding of blood there is no forgiveness (Hebrews 9:22, *NASB*).

He is so rich in kindness that he purchased our freedom through the blood of his Son, and our sins are forgiven (Ephesians 1:7, *NLT*).

💬 **Why do you think God chose to use blood—and the blood of His Son—to be the thing that cleanses us from sin?**

Do you know what Jesus' blood does for you? Let's take a look at Isaiah 1:18:

"Come now, let us reason together," says the LORD. "Though your sins are like scarlet, they shall be as white as snow; though they are red as crimson, they shall be like wool.

Most of us would probably think of blood as something that stains (I got blood on a white shirt the other day, and I'm not sure I'll be able to get the stain out), but God uses the blood of Jesus to *wash away* our stains and make us new again. So, whatever our sin—whatever stains have made their mark on our life—we can put them under the blood of Jesus, and they'll never be counted against us again.

God's Grace

According to the Merriam-Webster Online Dictionary, "mercy" implies compassion that forbears punishing even when justice demands it.[1] In other words, God, in His mercy, does not give us what we deserve. We deserve punishment and death for our sins, but because of the blood of Jesus, God extends mercy to us. Jesus took the punishment for our sins so that we don't have to. We will still face consequences and discipline for the wrong things we do, but we won't have to face eternal judgment for them.

Soul Sister: Trust

- **Describe a time when someone really hurt or offended you and you didn't give them what they deserved (in other words, you didn't strike back or try to get revenge).**

Grace is favor from God that we *do not* deserve. We've done nothing to deserve eternity with Christ or to deserve any of the blessings He's given us on Earth, but by the grace of God (a phrase that maybe you've heard thrown around), we have these things! So, not only does God *not* give us what we do deserve, but He also gives us good things that we are totally not deserving of. Amazing! We cannot earn His grace; we just have to open our arms wide and receive it.

In our world, we usually have to earn people's approval—we have to do something to show them we are worthy or cool to be accepted by them. We are liked because of how we perform or what we look like or what we can give, not usually just for who we are. God does just the opposite—He gives grace to the person who has done nothing and, actually, because of grace, makes that person into something!

- **Where do you see God's grace at work in your life? Write down specific examples.**

- **We should always strive to be like Christ. Think of someone who has done nothing to earn your friendship or your favor, and then think of something nice you can do for that person just to show them the love of Jesus. Who is that person and what will you do for him or her?**

not feelin' it?

Although forgiveness should spring out of love, it is not a feeling. This means that you do not have to *feel* love for someone in order to forgive him or her.

- What did Jesus say to Peter when Peter asked Him how often he should forgive someone who sins against him (see Matthew 18:21-22)?

- What do you think Jesus meant when He answered, "seventy-seven times"?

I don't know about you, but I'd be pretty ticked if I had to forgive someone 77 times! So what do you do when you feel annoyed with someone who does this or when you don't *feel* like forgiving at all? Here are a few ways that I handle situations in which there's a repeat offender or I'm just not feeling it.

1. Let It Go

Some things may annoy you or hurt your feelings, but they aren't offenses worth making a big deal over. Maybe you feel like somebody dissed you, or perhaps your best friend snapped at you on the phone. Don't let little offenses fester in your heart! Let them go! Pray and ask God to help you do that, and then release forgiveness to that person in your *heart* (again, there is no need to make an issue of something that the person has probably forgotten about or never knew he or she did in the first place). If you can't do that, then . . .

2. Talk About It

Communication is so, so important! First, talk about the problem with the Lord. Tell Him what the other person did to hurt you, and ask Him for wisdom in how to share your feelings with that person. Then talk to that person. It's easy to go to someone else in the name of venting to try to process your feelings, but that usually solves nothing (and it can really damage the relationship). If you need a third party's perspective, get it from a parent, mentor or older friend who's out of the picture. Also, pray to have grace and a kind spirit toward the person who wronged you.

> Write down Proverbs 16:21 and 24. What can you learn from those verses about the power of your words and how you should approach others?

3. Pray!

I know that I just mentioned this under item number 1 above, but I can't stress it enough. Whenever I feel offended by someone and I feel the threat of unforgiveness lurking in my heart, I go to God. I want to forgive the other person, but I also want to keep myself pure. I don't want bitterness and anger to grow inside me—that would make the problem far worse. When you seek God and ask Him to keep your heart soft and pure, He will protect you from becoming bitter. Remember, God is the author of forgiveness. He is able to heal you and help you work through even the worst hurts.

4. Get Help

Okay, I know that I just told you not to talk to anybody else first, but sometimes you need to seek out godly counsel to help you sort out tough issues. This is especially true if someone has harmed you in a physically or emotionally abusive way. Do *not* try to cope with abusive situations alone. Talk to a trusted adult. Proverbs 20:18 says, "Make plans by seeking advice; if you wage war, obtain guidance."

Forgiveness is not always easy, but it *is* always freeing—both for you and for the offender. As girls who are doing things God's way, you've got to keep a soft heart, be confident when you have to confront, and be gracious with everyone. Let's take a minute to pray and ask God to seal these things in our hearts and minds.

> Lord Jesus, thank You for the blood that You shed for me in order to bring me forgiveness. Thank You that my sins—past, present and future—are totally washed away. I receive Your forgiveness. Help me be a person who keeps a forgiving and kind heart toward others. Please give me the ability to do unto them as You have done to me. And help me to walk in the way of forgiveness. Amen.

Note

1. Merriam-Webster Online Dictionary, s.v. "mercy." http://www.m-w.com/dictionary/mercy (accessed June 8, 2006).

eight: friendship and forgiveness

He who covers over an offense promotes love, but whoever repeats the matter separates close friends.
Proverbs 17:9

A couple years ago, I had to talk to a friend about a serious issue in her life. We had been friends for about 14 years—nearly half our lives (as long as some of you are old!). We jokingly called ourselves "bridesmaids forever" (spoken with a true California valley girl accent: "Like, oh ma gosh, bridesmaids forever!"), believing that, one day, we would each be bridesmaids in each other's weddings. She was one of my nearest and dearest. Just a few months earlier, she had told me that there were only a few people in this world she could really trust—only two or three whom she really considered *best* friends. I was one of them.

- **Who are your nearest and dearest "bridesmaids forever" friends?**

- **Have any of them ever done anything to really hurt you?**

- **How did you respond?**

BEST FRIENDS forever?

This friend of mine—we'll call her Erica—said this to me when I was out of the country, so I wasn't living up close and personal with her. When I returned and actually stayed with her for a few weeks, I discovered that she had been sleeping with her boyfriend.

I agonized over confronting Erica on this issue because I had a strong sense that she did not want to hear it. But the Bible says that when we see a brother or sister sinning, we have to say something. Now, that doesn't mean we go around looking for all the faults in our friends. But when a friend's sin is repeated, is ruining her life (whether she admits it or not) and is dragging down the name of Jesus before others, we've got to speak up!

- Read Galatians 6:1. What does it say you should do when you catch a sister in sin? How are you to do that?

- What does Ephesians 5:11 say about this?

Wow, that's intense! The Ephesians verse takes on quite a different flavor from the Galatians one, doesn't it? Sounds as though the first thing we're supposed to do is try to gently bring a friend back onto the right path, but then, if she won't listen, we're not even supposed to hang out with the girl! I guess God means business.

Well, as I predicted, Erica did not take my "gentle redirecting" well—and I promise it was *gentle*. I mean, I can be an intense, straightforward person sometimes, but I tried to keep it mellow with her. I really wanted to see her set free from the lifestyle of immorality into which she had fallen. I was also a little perturbed that while she was living this way, she was still trying to get her boyfriend to go to church with her! Now *that's* a great witness!

So, anyway, long story short, she wrote me a harsh e-mail filled with all of the bad things she thought I was doing and telling me to stay out of her business. And so I did. We have e-mailed a few times since then, but it's been a couple years since we've really talked. I e-mailed her recently and asked if we could catch up, have coffee, nothing serious. She didn't reply.

Eight: Friendship and Forgiveness

All of this I've taken to the Lord and released to Him. I know I did what He wanted me to do from the start and that I tried to be a good friend. Her response hurt me deeply, but I forgave her and am ready to love her and take her back as a friend if she wants to come back. My greatest hope, however, is not that she'll be my friend again, but that she'll truly surrender her life to Jesus, receive His forgiveness, and walk in His ways.

- What would you have done in my situation?

- Write down some creative ways of working out a situation like this. Think about what Jesus might do in the situation.

top model

Who's watched *America's Next Top Model*? (Who's wanted to be *on* it??? C'mon, that's okay, you can admit it! At 14, I would have loved to do something like that, but my 5' 5" stature did not exactly win me a spot on the runway! Oh well . . .) More than just the beauty of these young aspiring models or the experiences they have, I think the entertainment value of the show—the thing that really sells it—is in watching the girls scratch each other's eyes out. It's called "cattiness," and without it, I don't think there'd be a show.

We've all seen it (whether on a reality show or in real life) and some of us have even experienced it: girls eyeing each other from head to toe, comparing themselves to one another, whispering to the girl next to them about another girl's frizzy hair (or wanna-be shoes, or unfriendly attitude, or stupid makeup—you get the idea). They want desperately to appear cool and confident, usually because everything inside them feels insecure.

How could there not be backbiting and jealousy on such a show where every girl has come to compete for such a coveted position? Each of them is under the microscope for weeks to determine who is the most beautiful, exotic, unique or photogenic. Their focus is on *self*, and whenever that's the case—especially with a group of women—look out! And it's not just the contestants who get catty and critical with each other. Most of the damage is done by the judges! Yes, they're paid to act like jerks, but—besides a fat paycheck for them—what good comes out of it?

- Here's a project for you that might take some time, but at least you don't have to make a special trip. Grab a small notebook and a pen and keep it with you when you go to school, to the mall, or anywhere there might be a large gathering of girls or women. Find a place where you can quietly and casually observe a group of girls. Watch how they watch other girls and note what they say to their friends when a particularly pretty or a particularly different girl walks by. If you're close enough to hear them (not that I encourage eavesdropping), take notes on that, too. You can even do this (discreetly!) while hanging with your own homegirls.

- Were the girls you watched cool or catty? Did anything you observed strike you as ugly behavior? Were you surprised by anything you saw or heard?

- Read Ephesians 5:13-16. What does verse 15 say about catty behavior?

So, what does this have to do with forgiveness? I'm glad you asked. Being a forgiving person—and a good friend—not only means that you love and forgive those who hurt you but also that you walk in forgiveness on a daily basis. Remember, "While we were still sinners, Christ died for us" (Romans 5:8). Regardless of your relationship with a person (or if you even know them at all), you need to have a gracious, kind attitude toward them.

Jesus was friendly toward the outcasts He met. He didn't cop an attitude on anybody. If He had something harsh to say, He said it directly, speaking the truth in love. Our lives must pattern His, and that means having His heart of forgiveness toward all people.

Eight: Friendship and Forgiveness

working it out

Read what Matthew 18:15-17 states about what we're to do when someone hurts or offends us:

> If a fellow believer hurts you, go and tell him—work it out between the two of you. If he listens, you've made a friend. If he won't listen, take one or two others along so that the presence of witnesses will keep things honest, and try again. If he still won't listen, tell the church. If he won't listen to the church, you'll have to start over from scratch, confront him with the need for repentance, and offer again God's forgiving love (*THE MESSAGE*).

Sometimes, an offense isn't so easy to overcome. When people hurt me, I feel as though they should know what they did and come and apologize to me. Can you relate? But this doesn't often happen. Usually, it's the one who feels offended who has to go to the offender to try to make things right—to make reconciliation.

Just in the last 24 hours, two situations—not one, but *two*—have brought me face to face with the question of forgiveness *and* surrender. How appropriate is that?! (Okay, Lord, I get it; You're testing me to see if I'm just blowing smoke or really walking the talk here.)

One of these situations was with my roommate. She and I are *very* different. She's really laid back, whereas I'm a little more structured and disciplined. I'm also a very light sleeper, so it's hard for me to get back to sleep if someone wakes me up (whereas she has slept through a fire alarm going off right outside her door!). Well . . . at about midnight, I hear the phone ringing, but I don't answer it in time. Then I hear someone banging on the front door. I don't get up to answer it. Finally, I hear a key in the lock—it's my roommate, coming in late from a weekend away. I figure out immediately what has happened: She couldn't find her keys, so she woke me up to let her in. No big deal, right? I mean, that's what roommates do for each other. But this was about the third or fourth time something like this had happened since we had been living together. Grrr!

The second situation was with a new friend whom I've spent some time with lately. We were talking on the phone, and the conversation got a bit sarcastic. I love to joke around, but I'm not big into being sarcastic; it doesn't really build people up, and it often carries with it an element of disrespect. If taken too far—even in the name of fun—feelings can get hurt. That's exactly what happened. *My* feelings got hurt. To top it off, his phone died, mid-joke (actually while he was laughing at me). I know he didn't mean to hang up on me, but I have to admit that I felt a bit rejected. It felt as if he wasn't really respecting me.

With both situations came a true test of my character: Would I surrender my pride and feelings of rejection and irritation and tell these two people what got to me? Would I forgive them despite their disrespect toward me and despite what their responses might be? Well, I didn't exactly have to drag my friends before the church or bring another person along with me, but I did have to go to them first.

When my roommate woke up the next morning, I asked her—graciously—about the situation and told her that I couldn't get back to sleep after her little misplaced-key incident. I asked her to please be more responsible with her keys so that she wouldn't get in a bind again. She wasn't too receptive at first. She thought that I was making too big a deal out of nothing, but a few minutes later she came back and apologized for being inconsiderate. I also apologized to her for being edgy and annoyed.

With the boy, well, that was a little different. I was kind of nervous. I didn't want to get all serious on him and have him think, *This girl's a trip! Too emotional for me.* But I also couldn't just pretend that everything was okay. So I e-mailed him the next day and told him how I felt, that I had felt a little hurt by his behavior. It turns out that he had no idea he had offended me and wanted me to know that he felt terrible for it.

The great thing about both of these situations is that my friends understand me a bit better now, and vice versa. No hidden tension, no festering irritation, no temptation to run out and talk about the other person behind his or her back.

Maybe you've heard that the skin of a scar is tougher than the skin that was there before the skin was cut. Well, the same is true with relationships. Sticky situations, when handled with grace and forgiveness, can often be the things that really strengthen them.

Let's pray.

> Lord Jesus, I want to have a heart of forgiveness like You have. Help me to love my friends, to be real with them and to forgive them if they hurt me. Help me, too, to be humble and ask for forgiveness when I offend someone. I want to be a shining example to everyone around me that offenses don't have to ruin relationships but can actually strengthen them. In Jesus' name, amen.

If there's any friend in your life that you've held back from forgiving or anyone whom you need to ask to forgive you for anything, pray right now and ask the Lord to help you do this. He will! He'll give you the right words to say to that person. Don't delay—make that relationship right, right away!

nine: Honor and Respect

A gracious woman attains honor.
Proverbs 16:11, *NASB*

A kindhearted woman gains respect.
Proverbs 16:11

A woman of gentle grace gets respect.
Proverbs 16:11, *THE MESSAGE*

Would others say that you have high self-esteem? That you truly like who you are and love being yourself? If you do, *beautiful*! But too many girls, when they get into their teens, become dissatisfied with the way they look and become self-conscious about everything from their weight to being seen in public with their parents. They compare themselves to other girls, which makes them feel insecure about who they are and who God created them to be.

Such insecurities give way to a lack of self-respect. Without self-respect, we're likely to do things to try to make other people think we're cool and to look to guys to give us a sense of worth and acceptance. Without self-respect, it's hard to respect people in authority over us too, such as parents and teachers.

Where, then, do we ultimately gain a sense of personal worth and value and the self-respect that enables us to honor and respect others? Having a happy home life contributes to it, as does having solid relationships with other soul sisters. However, there's something more, something deeper, something at the foundation of all the rest.

IMAGO DEI

Genesis 1:27 states, "So God created man in his own image, in the image of God he created him; male and female he created them." Did you know that you are created in the very image of God? Did you know that the very fingers of God formed you (see Psalm 139:13-16*)*? That, in Latin, is called *imago Dei*, or the "image of God."

Respect for yourself begins in knowing that God Himself created you for Himself. In fact, not only did He create you, but He also crafted and fashioned you. Like a skillful artist, He delighted in making every detail of you. I'm not just talking about your physical appearance— I'm talking about your *spirit* and your *soul*, the very essence of you. Your worth comes from Him, and your value is in Him.

- Grab that journal of yours (or use the space provided here) and answer this question: What about *me* is unique? Think of everything from your laugh to your eye color to your particular interests and quirks. Don't be ashamed! Go ahead, write these things down!

- Now circle your top five favorite things about yourself from that list.

- How does it make you feel to know that God created you to be uniquely you?

- Think about your particular gifts and abilities. Write down two or three. How can you use those gifts and abilities to serve others and to serve God's greater purpose in the world?

See, that's another thing that God gives to you: *purpose*. He created you purposefully and intentionally. Even if your parents called you a "surprise" or one or both of them abandoned you, God gave you life. He has a reason (many reasons, in fact!) for you to be alive today.

Consider two of my Brazilian friends: Tatiana and Viviane. Both of their mothers were prostitutes, and neither of them knew their fathers. Viviane's mom even tried to abort her. Did Vivi have to deal with serious issues of rejection in her life? Absolutely. Did she have to learn to forgive her mother (and father) for wanting to kill her? Most definitely. Was it easy? Not in the least. But she did it. She forgave her parents and ended up becoming a talented, funny young woman who now travels the world ministering with her American husband and their two sons.

Although Tatiana's mom didn't attempt to abort her, she didn't provide the most stable, loving home life for her children. At a young age, Tatiana became involved with drugs and guys, which led her into depression and a desire to end her life. While I won't go into her story here, I will say that God rescued her in a dramatic way. She has since become a semiprofessional dancer and a passionate preacher of the gospel. Today, she lives in New Zealand with her husband and their two beautiful daughters.

reflecting AND deflecting

With that in mind—that God is passionate about you and has an amazing purpose for your life—you can rest assured in your own self-worth and begin to focus on pouring yourself out for others. Let's do a little Bible study to find out God's way of doing this.

- Get your Bible and read Philippians 2:3 and Romans 12:10. In light of these Scriptures, who are you to consider first: yourself or others?

- How does considering someone else's preferences above your own show them honor? Give a specific example.

- What does Hebrews 2:7 say about the place of honor God intended for all people?

- What's the take on all of this in 1 Peter 2:17?

In Luke 18:20, Jesus mentions the Ten Commandments, which are found in Exodus 20:12-17. What seems to be the underlying principle of each and every commandment? Honor God and respect others, right? If that's the foundation of something as important as the Ten Commandments, this should tell us that God places extreme value on honoring and esteeming other people above ourselves.

- **How are you doing in this department? List a few ways in which you're good at honoring others.**

- **List areas in which you could work on the respect factor.**

In a nutshell, the art of respect lies in learning to *reflect* the light of Christ from yourself—drawing attention to Him—and to *deflect* attention from yourself onto others.

guys

Honoring others also means honoring your brothers in the Lord. Giving guys respect will earn their respect for you. They might not realize it at the time, but subconsciously they will respect you, and over time, you'll gain a reputation for being one cool, confident chick.

What do I mean by this? How does it play out? Well, perhaps a better way to illustrate this is by giving you an example of what it's not.

When I was 13, no one really told me how to interact with guys. I respected my dad—I feared him, in a good way, because he was a pretty tough disciplinarian—and I didn't have much to do with my brother (except, of course, for the occasional spat). I didn't realize that having respect for myself wasn't just about me and my personal purity but also about the guys around me.

Unfortunately, I craved their attention. Too often, I compromised my own standards and self-respect to get that attention. In doing so, not only was I disrespecting myself, but I was also disrespecting them as well. I was not helping them guard their hearts.

Proverbs 4:23 tells us to guard our heart above all else. I think we can carry that into guarding the hearts of others too—making sure that we don't mislead them or lead them into hurtful situations. As God's girls, we ought to consider guys' hearts and feelings above our own (guys' hearts get broken too, ya know!). We also ought to do everything in our power to protect their purity. After all, the most loving thing we can do for any person, whether male or female or old or young, is to show them a shining example of who Christ is.

💬 **What advice does Paul give Timothy about this in 1 Timothy 5:1-2 and 1 Timothy 4:12?**

THE FIFTH COMMANDMENT

In Exodus 20:12, God gives the command to honor our parents. It is number 5 out of 10 (it even comes before "Thou shall not murder"!).

💬 **Why do you think honoring our parents is such an important thing to God?**

💬 **What does it say about us when we honor and obey our parents (especially publicly)? What about when we don't respect them?**

Let's be real here: Not everybody has the greatest parents. Not everyone has parents who have stuck around or really been there for him or her. Many kids get wounded and scarred by parents who are living out of their own hurt, fear and insecurity. If this is your story, God the Father is here to heal you. He will be a loving parent to you and can bring older men and women into your life to provide some of the support and guidance that your parents didn't give you.

Remember my friend Tatiana? When she came to the United States, God brought two very important people into her life: Bill and Cathie, the leaders of the ministry that she and I toured with for several years. They became second parents to her. They were the ones who counseled her before she got married. They were the ones who were there when she had her first child. They are the ones who she comes home to when she visits the United States. Over the years, Tati has reconciled with her real mother—she's forgiven her, and they've established a good relationship. Bill and Cathie, however, remain her spiritual parents, her home away from home.

If you have a dysfunctional relationship with your folks, you are not exempt from respecting them. This is a challenge, but it's a command that, if kept, will be rewarded. If this is your situation, pause for a minute to pray and ask the Lord to help you forgive your mom and/or dad. Ask Him to give you the grace to respect them and love them despite the things they've done to hurt you. Ask Him also to bring other adults into your life that you can trust and respect.

- **Write down your frustrations with your parents.**

- **Write down how you will forgive them.**

- **Now write down your personal commitment to honor and respect them from here on out.**

I, thankfully, don't have too much to complain about my parents. Things weren't perfect, but I always felt loved, safe and provided for. Now, as an adult, I'm convinced that God blessed me with two of the best parents on the planet! But does that mean I always respected them? Nooo!

It must be a total shock for some moms to go from holding their little girl's hand all the time to suddenly being given the hand "because the face ain't listenin'!" I'm sure I did that to my mom many times. I'm sure I rolled my eyes at her. I'm sure I hurt her feelings a lot along the way.

My dad? Well, I couldn't quite get away with rolling my eyes at him, but I did lie to him (as you read about in session 1), and I showed him disrespect in various other ways. God says this is a sin.

Nine: Honor and Respect

💬 **What does God say about respecting our parents in Proverbs 20:20 and 30:17?**

Scary! Snuffed out in pitch darkness? Eyes pecked out by birds and eaten by vultures? God sure isn't afraid to be graphic when He wants to get a message across, is He?!

Well, my dears, one of the reasons that respect for your parents—and for anyone in authority over you (teachers, bosses, pastors, police officers, and so forth)—is so crucial is because it directly reflects the respect you have for God. And that is above all most important. Is God our friend? Yes. Does He want us to know that we are unconditionally loved? Yes. But He is also to be feared, to be revered. He is, plainly speaking, the King of the Universe and deserving of all honor and respect.

💬 **Before we close this session, take a few minutes to read the following verses:**

1 Corinthians 6:20

Isaiah 29:13

Proverbs 3:9

💬 **Based on these verses, what are three specific ways you can show respect and honor for God?**

Let's pray.

Lord, I commit to honoring You with all of myself. I pray that honor for You will overflow into every relationship I have. Help me to be a woman of honor, to have self-respect and to respect others the way Jesus did. In His name, amen.

TEN: Mirror, Mirror, on the Wall...

Why do you look at the speck of sawdust in your brother's eye and pay no attention to the plank in your own eye? How can you say to your brother, "Brother, let me take the speck out of your eye," when you yourself fail to see the plank in your own eye? You hypocrite, first take the plank out of your eye, and then you will see clearly to remove the speck from your brother's eye.

Luke 6:41-42

Have you looked in a mirror lately? My guess is you probably have. I *know* that I have—about 200 times in the last 24 hours! Yeah, it's that vanity thing that we criticize the girls on *America's Next Top Model* for. Oops—maybe we don't have much room to talk after all! Maybe it's time for us to look past the face in the mirror and examine what's going on in the heart.

A LESSON FROM THE STARS

I'm browsing through a popular women's magazine right now—a magazine that just a couple decades ago would have been considered pornographic. Half of the eight cover articles have to do with sex, two are about getting what you want from others, one is about a movie star, and one is about never having a zit again.

- **Grab the nearest fashion magazine you can find. Flip through its pages for a few minutes. What is the focus of nearly every page and every article? (Even glimpsing at the table of contents will give you an idea of what I'm getting at here.) In the space below, jot down some of your observations.**

Lust, vanity, fame, "me first" messages—what does all of this point to? *Self.* There's even a magazine titled exactly that! And these messages are not only found in popular magazines. Think of some of the music you hear on the radio—maybe even a few of your favorite songs. What do you think is the focus of most mainstream music (and even of some Christian music)?

- **Write down the names of three popular or favorite secular songs in the space below.**

- **Now listen to the lyrics of those songs. Write down any words that are repeated over and over. What seems to be the main point?**

Well, *my* point is that so much music is also about *self*. The singer wants that girl to satisfy his lust or that guy to love her. So much of it is about what the other person does to please him or her. I can't say that I've heard too many songs lately on secular stations in Seattle that talk about selflessness and serving others!

A friend and I were talking about selfishness the other night—about how selfishness is at the core of all sin. Whether you want to protect yourself from looking bad (pride), or you hurt someone else to get what you want, or you give in to some physical desire (food, lust) to try to fulfill yourself, it's all about one two-letter word: "me."

A friend of mine was preparing to preach the gospel on a few university campuses and was thinking about how to help people realize their sinfulness by showing them their selfishness. As I thought more about it, this is what came to mind—it's from an e-mail I sent to him the next day:

> Hey! Good talking to you last night!
> I've thought more about the subject of selfishness and something came to mind—something that's often made me think about the futility of fame. So, we see these people striving after fame—Brittany, Madonna, J-Lo, Jessica Simpson, Brad Pitt—(and who doesn't want to be rich and famous, right?), but that is not enough for them. Especially with the female singers. They get to the top of the charts, and that's not enough; and a movie and a clothing line and a fragrance line aren't enough; and being a sex goddess and compromising everything they used to be isn't enough, so they have to get a man (and often someone else's

man). And the media makes a big deal about them "getting married." Then that's not enough; they have to have a baby. (Who knows, hopefully having a baby to take care of will help them focus a little less on themselves!)

It's that thing you talked about last night, the lust that's never satisfied. But it's all about (so it seems) the satisfaction of self. At the end of this selfish pursuit, sadly, suicide is the final selfish act for some famous ones. It's just an interesting observation and might be something worth pointing out to those students who live vicariously through their favorite hip-hop star. None of it satisfies.

get real!

Alright, ladies, let's be honest about our own dirt. Actually, I've already bared some of the dark secrets of my past to you. Now it's your turn to fess up and get real about your sinful condition.

- **It's easy to pick out the flaws in other people, but what do the following Scriptures communicate about recognizing our own sinfulness?**

You, therefore, have no excuse, you who pass judgment on someone else, for at whatever point you judge the other, you are condemning yourself, because you who pass judgment do the same things (Romans 2:1).

We all, like sheep, have gone astray, each of us has turned to his own way (Isaiah 53:6).

As it is written: "There is no one righteous, not even one; there is no one who . . . seeks God. All have turned away . . . there is no one who does good" (Romans 3:10-12).

Why do you look at the speck of sawdust in your brother's eye and pay no attention to the plank in your own eye? How can you say to your brother, "Brother, let me take the speck out of your eye," when you yourself fail to see the plank in your own eye? You hypocrite, first take the plank out of your eye, and then you will see clearly to remove the speck from your brother's eye (Luke 6:41-42).

Getting real is the first step to getting free. We start by letting God into those ugly areas of our lives—whether they're in the deep recesses of our hearts or out there on the surface (usually where everyone but us can see them!). Of course, He already knows our hearts and every little thing we've ever done, but He wants *us* to confess our sins directly to Him. He wants *us* to take responsibility for our bad behaviors, our wrong motives, our failures to love others. God wants the real us to step forward and confess our sins from the heart!

- **Have you been real with yourself lately? Have you been real with God? Search your soul. Are there any selfish ways or unconfessed sins taking up space in there? Write them down.**

- **Have you asked God to forgive you for these things? Do you believe that He does? Do you forgive yourself?**

First John 1:9 says, "If we confess our sins, he is faithful and just and will forgive us our sins and purify us from all unrighteousness." It is in recognizing and confessing our sins that true forgiveness is found and real repentance begins. Even our darkest deeds can be washed away by the blood of Jesus! When they are, we become whiter than snow.

- **Read Psalm 51:7 and Hebrews 10:22. What do these Scriptures say to you?**

Remember in session 7 when we talked about the power of blood? The blood of Jesus is the ultimate purifier. No stain can withstand it! The only thing that can withstand the blood of Jesus is the will that chooses not to receive it.

from the wicked witch to snow white

Do you remember the story of Snow White? She was a princess whose evil stepmother, the queen, became jealous of her surpassing beauty. She made Snow White slave at chores until, finally, unable to control her jealousy, she sent her out into the woods to be killed by a huntsman. When that plan failed, the evil queen herself went out and put a poisoned apple in Snow White's possession. As the story goes, of course, Snow White ate the apple and fell into a deathlike state until her prince found her and kissed her back to life again.

As with the evil queen in Snow White, at the heart of human nature is the desire to be told, "You are the fairest one of all!" We know that this is especially the case with women! It's interesting to note, too, that this is the very reason why Satan fell from glory—he wanted to be the most beautiful, most admired, most adored, most worshiped. His self-centeredness caused him to become the most evil being in the universe.

> **How often have you wished that all eyes were on you? Have you wanted to be the most popular or most beautiful girl and maybe, perhaps, been jealous of the ones who appeared to be that?**

If we're honest with ourselves, we'll see that we also have the tendency to want to be the center of everyone else's world. We'll see that we have a seed of selfishness—called sin—that causes us to act like a wicked witch sometimes. It's that seed that eventually causes all people to fall into, not just a deathlike state, but death itself.

But in this version of the story, we're all like the Wicked Witch (Evil Queen, Cruella Deville, Darth Vader—name your villain). We've all hurt others, we've all wanted the magic mirror to worship us, we've all taken a bite out of the forbidden fruit. Only one thing can save us. Only the kiss of Jesus, the drops of His blood, can awaken us from our mortal slumber and release us from sin's power.

Let's pray.

Father God, search my heart. See if there is any wicked thing in me. I confess to You now the things that I know have offended You. I need Your forgiveness, and I receive it! I also need Your help to overcome the sinful areas in my life. I want to turn away from looking at myself and look to You. I want to look outward to think more about the needs of others. Thank You that, together with You, I can do this! I love You!

eleven: tough love

So watch yourselves. If your brother sins, rebuke him, and if he repents, forgive him.
Luke 17:3

Short, sweet, to the point: If your friend sins, rebuke her; if she repents, forgive her. This is Jesus' simple formula for getting friends back on the right track. Tell 'em, love 'em, and get on with it.

So what does it mean to rebuke someone, anyway? Well, perhaps a better definition for our purposes is one from one of its synonyms, "reprove," which means "to scold or correct usually gently or with kindly intent."[1]

- **Have you had to rebuke or reprove anyone lately?**

- **If so, how did you feel before you said something to that person? How did you feel afterward?**

- **Has anyone rebuked you lately? If so, what was the outcome of the situation?**

Real love is often tough love—and tough love requires courage and communication. It requires honesty and humility. It requires a desire to see your loved ones (and yourself) set free from sin more than you desire to be liked and accepted.

77

THE COURAGE TO FAIL

Remember my story about my friend Erica whom I confronted and lost because she couldn't let go of her sinful lifestyle? Do you think that I failed because we're no longer friends? Sure, I could have done things differently—and probably better—but I did the best I could and, most important, I did it in love.

> What does the first sentence of 1 Corinthians 13:8 say on this subject?

    I approached my friend in love, yet it seems as if it was a failure. Hmm . . . but, no, love didn't fail—and I didn't fail—the approach of love is always the winning way. While we can't control the outcome of situations or the free will of others, we can control how we speak and respond to them. And when we care enough to confront our friends in love for something they've done to hurt us or for a sinful pattern we see them walking in, we are successful in God's sight!

    Are you willing to take that risk? Are you willing to put honesty, integrity and godly concern above the possibility of rejection? You won't always get the words out right and or say everything exactly the way you'd planned, but you need to have the courage to "fail" and try again.

> Look up the following verses and rewrite each one in your own words:
>
>   Proverbs 27:6
>
>   Ecclesiastes 4:10
>
>   Matthew 18:15

> What stood out to you most in these passages?

James 5:20 says, "Remember this: Whoever turns a sinner from the error of his way will save him from death and cover over a multitude of sins." Wow! Save somebody from death?! Cover a multitude of sins?! This verse alone encourages me to be a speaker of truth and to be one who boldly attempts to rescue friends who might otherwise go down in flames!

a lesson from the guys

Have you ever noticed the way guys communicate? I mean, in general, they say what they mean to each other (or they don't say anything at all!) and they don't get catty about it. They just don't seem to take things as personally as we girls do. It might go something like this:

> "Hey, look, you're an awesome man of God, and I totally see your heart, but you've been a little too friendly with some of the ladies lately. I know you're just trying to be a friend, but a couple girls are taking it the wrong way."
> And his friend might say: "Seriously? Oh, I had no idea. Hmm. Okay, yeah, I'll watch out for that."
> Or he might say, "Seriously? Dude, I think you're making too big of a deal out of nothing. They're the ones always coming up to me."

Either way, whether the rebuke is accepted or not, the conversations (of the guys I know, at least) usually seem to end on a positive note. It's like they change the subject and start talking about sports or decide to go play X-Box or something. We girls, on the other hand, would be like, "No way! I'm not going shopping with her! She totally just got in my face!" (Okay, maybe you're not that bad, but you get my point, right?). Even when I've seen guys take offense, they still manage to be friends the next day.

Anyway, so I've learned to play hardball the boy's way. I try not to get too emotional when I bring things up with a girlfriend—or a guy friend or a family member, for that matter. I pray about what I need to say and wait to say it until my emotions are submitted to my spirit and under control. I try not to be too emotional, but I do take others' emotions into account—so my approach looks different with each person. I don't slam or throw out hurtful comments—my goal isn't to make the other person feel bad but to remedy the situation.

If the other person is angry or flips out on me, I try to stay calm. I look the person in the eye and try to bring some encouragement and light to the situation, while still speaking the truth. I try not to worry about what that individual thinks of me and whether he or she will still like me—because it's not all about me.

💬 What have you noticed about the way guys communicate?

💬 What's the hardest thing for you when it comes to confronting someone you love?

THE SANDWICH RULE

Let's look back at our definition for "rebuke" (or "reprove"). Correction is the first half of it, but a super direct approach doesn't usually do much to bring about change. Being straightforward is good, but it requires grace. Correction served "gently or with kindly intent" is much better received than correction delivered raw to the heart of the receiver.

Here's something for you to try: Go into your kitchen and pull the peanut butter and jam out of the fridge (or marmot, Nutella, mayonnaise, mustard—whatever gooey thing you normally like to eat on a piece of bread). Now take your PB and J (or whatever) and spread it on the palm of your hand. Go ahead, do it! Spread that thing all over your hand like you'd spread it on a piece of bread! Now add a few other favorite things to your "hand sandwich." Cheese? Turkey? Tomato? Honey? Your choice, pile it on! Are you done yet? Okay, now eat it. That's right, eat the stuff right off your hand! Fun? Messy? A little difficult, maybe?

This is kind of what it's like when we try to bring correction without encouragement. It's messy, it's awkward, and it's difficult to do. It just doesn't feel right. And there's usually a much bigger mess to clean up after the job is done. So, a good rule of thumb to follow when faced with confronting someone is the sandwich rule:

1. Start with something good ("Haley, you're such a good friend. I really appreciate what a good listener you are.").

2. Then add the "meat" of your message—the tough stuff ("But I've noticed how you sometimes gossip about what other people tell you. As your friend, I need to tell you that it's hurting people and making you look bad. It's getting hard for me to trust you, too.").

3. Close it with grace ("Anyway, I'm saying this to you because I care about you and I care about our friendship and your other friendships. You really are an amazing friend.").

Ta da! Something like that. Confrontation is never easy—it must be preceded by faith and prayer (don't forget that all-important detail!)—but it can be done.

confess it now!

What about our own sin? What about when we need to be honest with someone about the things we have done? Sometimes our sins are obvious—they cry out for us to address them—but many times they are hidden. We feel embarrassed and ashamed by the things we've done or the thoughts we've had, and we feel as though we are the only one who has ever done them. If that's the case, we reason, how can we tell a soul about these shameful secrets?!

Sexual sin is especially easy to hide and especially hard to confess. But, please, I plead with you right now, if you have a secret sexual sin, whether it's a continuous thing or something that happened six weeks ago, *confess it now*! Don't wait. First Corinthians 6:18 tells us to "flee from sexual immorality," saying that it is a sin against our very own bodies.

If this is you—whether you've had sex, you've gone too far, you find yourself having sexual fantasies, or whatever—find a woman you trust and go talk with her about it. Again, as always, ask God for forgiveness and healing, but also talk it over with a godly woman. And memorize James 5:16: "Therefore confess your sins to each other and pray for each other so that you may be healed. The prayer of a righteous man is powerful and effective."

- What happens when you confess your sins to someone else and she prays for you?

- Do you believe that your prayers for others are "powerful and effective"?

- Do you have the courage to communicate your weaknesses and struggles to another soul sister? Write down the names of three friends to whom you think you could bare your soul.

A CLOSING WORD

An appropriate way to end this session is with a reminder of how vast, deep and wide God's love is for you. With Him, mercy triumphs over judgment. He longs to be gracious to you; therefore, you ought to be gracious toward others. Let's close with a word of Scripture and prayer:

> Above all, love each other deeply, because love covers over a multitude of sins (1 Peter 4:8).

> Dear Lord, thank You for the faithful friends You have given me. Thank You for the godly people in my life. I pray that You would give me the courage to speak up when I see a friend falling away from You. I also ask that You would help me be honest about my own sin. I commit to communicating well and to communicating courageously. I can do it all in Your name. Amen.

Note

1. Merriam-Webster Online Dictionary, s.v. "reprove." http://www.merriam-webster.com/dictionary/reprove (accessed June 11, 2006)

twelve: forgive
because you have been forgiven

He who covers over an offense promotes love, but whoever repeats the matter separates close friends.
Proverbs 17:9

AMAZING LOVE

I really enjoy old hymns. It's been years since I've gone to a church that sings hymns much, but I'm still drawn to them. They hold a richness that many contemporary worship songs seem to lack (but I love those as well, don't get me wrong—I mean, worship is worship!). Maybe it's my literary side.

On a side note, if you're not familiar with many (or any) hymns, I encourage you to Google "hymns" next time you're online and see what comes up. There's some really deep stuff in some of these songs that are hundreds of years old. Our spiritual ancestors knew what was up when they wrote the spoken word of their day!

One in particular really grabs me. It's called "And Can It Be," and it was written nearly 300 years ago by Charles Wesley. Now, it has some "thee"s and "thou"s in it, but try to get past those and just let the lyrics sink in:

> And can it be that I should gain
> An interest in the Savior's blood?
> Died He for me, who caused His pain—
> For me, who Him to death pursued?
> Amazing Love! How can it be,
> That Thou, my God, shouldst die for me?
> Amazing Love! How can it be,
> That Thou, my God, shouldst die for me?[1]

Mr. Wesley was spot-on with this one—Jesus died for *me*, who caused *His pain*. My sin and your sin drove Jesus to the cross. Of course, He had a choice in the matter; He didn't have to do it, but He did. Why? Because of His amazing love for you and for me! Amazing love, how can it be, that You, God of the universe, would die for *me*?!

This amazing love is the basis for our forgiveness. I don't know if we'll ever fully understand how great Jesus' sacrifice was and how great His pain was as He let Himself be crucified for us. What I do know is that forgiveness is now a gift for you and me to freely take.

TAKE 'N' GIVE

"Freely you have received, freely give," Jesus said in Matthew 10:8. While forgiveness from God is free for us—meaning we did not and cannot do anything to earn or deserve it—it comes with a responsibility: We must give it freely to others.

Centuries ago—and centuries apart from each other—there lived 2 young men. One was the youngest of 10 brothers and 1 of only 2 sons his father had with his second (and most beloved) wife. The other was the youngest of 7 brothers. Both of these men were singled out by the Lord to do something amazing with their lives, but before their season of greatness came, both were persecuted by the people closest to them.

The first man was Joseph. Jealous of their father's love for Joseph and angry with the dreams he was having and sharing (dreams about one day ruling over them), his brothers sold him as a slave and told their father that a wild beast had killed him. In the years that followed, Joseph lived as a slave and as a prisoner. He suffered these things before—by God's sovereign plan—becoming Pharaoh's right-hand man.

After God placed Joseph in this position of power, a severe famine hit the land. The famine was so bad that it drove Joseph's brothers to Egypt to find food. When Joseph saw them, it must have shocked his socks . . . er, I mean, sandals . . . off. After all these years, here were his brothers—who had sold him into slavery—bowing before him!

> Read Genesis 42:6-8; 42:21-25. What is Joseph's reaction when he first sees his brothers?

> Read Genesis 45. What is Joseph's ultimate response to these men who had once betrayed him?

Twelve: Forgive Because You Have Been Forgiven

I am so moved (I have tears in my eyes right now!) by verse 5: "Now do not be grieved or angry with yourselves, because you sold me here, for God sent me before you to preserve life" (*NASB*). This, my friends, is a beautiful picture of true forgiveness.

I don't know about you, but I wouldn't be too happy with my siblings if they sold me into slavery. But Joe, he doesn't just say, "Alright guys, I forgive you. Now where's Dad?" He gives them food and clothes and money and a whole new land to live in. He doesn't scold them for their past—doesn't even mention it—except to say that it was all part of God's will for his life and theirs. He glorifies God, gives attention to the good and gladly receives his brothers back into his life. This is truly amazing love.

IMPRISONMENT

Take a look again at Proverbs 17:9: "He who covers over an offense promotes love, but whoever repeats the matter separates close friends."

- **Did Joseph repeat or cover the crime his brothers committed against him?**

- **What happens when we hold on to bitterness—when we hold grudges against people for hurting us?**

Remember the parable we talked about in session 7—the story about the two slaves? At the end of that story, the king threw the first slave into prison after he saw his unforgiving behavior toward the other slave. When we refuse to forgive, we become like that slave. Our own bitterness imprisons us. When we won't release forgiveness to others, we ourselves can't be released.

- **Read Matthew 6:12-15. What is Jesus saying in these verses?**

Soul Sister: Trust

- **Read Luke 23:34. What kind of example did Jesus set for us even as He was dying on the cross?**

liberating love

In Luke 7:36-48, as Jesus was eating dinner in a house, a woman suddenly walked in with a jar of perfume, wet his feet with her tears, kissed them and poured perfume on them. Immediately, some of the people around Jesus began to make comments about her. "If this man were a prophet," one person said, "he would know who is touching him and what kind of woman she is—that she is a sinner" (v. 39).

- **Read Luke 7:44-46. How did Jesus respond to this accusation about the woman?**

- **What did Jesus say to defend her (v. 47)?**

Now that's a liberating kind of love! This woman had walked right into someone else's party, fallen at Jesus' feet and poured her heart out to Him with her tears and her oil and her hair. From what we see in this passage, it appears that she didn't even give a second glance at the other guys who were staring at her, gossiping about her.

At the beginning of this session, I said that there were two young men whom God used mightily but who also experienced rejection and hatred from people close to them. The second man was David—King David.

As a teen, God anointed David king in front of his seven older brothers (see 1 Samuel 16). But he didn't come into that position right away. Like Joseph, he had some understanding of what lay ahead, but first he had to walk through some hard times.

Immediately after killing Goliath, David went into King Saul's service. At first, Saul delighted in David, but when he heard people singing David's praises over his own, he began to burn

Twelve: Forgive Because You Have Been Forgiven

with jealousy. That jealousy soon turned to rage, and that rage let Satan gain serious control over Saul's life (read 1 Samuel 18 and 19 to find out more). Over the next several years, Saul sought to take David's life. Yet David did not retaliate.

💬 **Read 1 Samuel 24. What did David do when given the opportunity to take revenge on Saul?**

This not only happened once but twice! Twice David had the chance to take Saul's life. Because he didn't, God exalted David.

The same is true with us. When we act with honor and integrity and turn from taking revenge on others, God honors us. When we forgive, even when no one asks us to (and even when others continue to wrong us) we—ultimately—are blessed.

Forgiveness brings freedom! Accepting God's forgiveness frees us. Turning and lavishing that forgiveness on others—even though it's difficult—takes us to a whole new level.

💬 **What has your response been to great forgiveness God has given you? Are you one who readily forgives others?**

SOMETHING FUN TO FINISH WITH...

Wow, so we're already at the end of the road. That went fast! Actually, you're only at the beginning—or somewhere along the way—of a very exciting journey of faith, freedom and continuing surrender and forgiveness.

What have you learned throughout our 12 sessions together? If you still have your collage journal around somewhere, pick it up and take a few minutes to sum up what spoke to you the most during this study.

When you're done with that, gather back together with your group (if you're in one) and get ready to brainstorm, because *I* have something for you to do in response to all this!

Remember my friends May and Louie, from session 4? Even as I write, those two and a team of others are planning two more events: a volleyball tournament and a young women's

Soul Sister: Trust

conference! I'm impressed by their creativity and inspired by their "just do it!" mentality.

Now, what can *you* do? Do you like to act, read, play basketball? Together with your group (or with another group of soul sisters, if you have done this study alone), brainstorm ideas for a small (or big!) outreach. It should be something that you can all pull off together, something that will bring unbelievers in and introduce them to Jesus and the forgiveness and freedom they can find in Him. It could be a café night (at a real café or at someone's house) with live music and art and people sharing their testimonies. Or it could be something much smaller, such as getting a few girls (saved and not-yet-saved) together for an overnighter, a hike or a concert.

Write your ideas down in your collage journal, a notebook or on a blank sheet of paper and then fill in the details. Make sure you include the following:

What? (What's your event?)
Where? (Specific location)
When? (Date/time)
Who? (Who are the organizers, what is each person's responsibility, and who are you going to invite?)
How? (How are you going to get the word out? How are you going to pay for it, if necessary? How is it all going to work—the details!?)

Once you have these things written down, make sure you have an adviser or a couple of adults who can help you (such as your group leader, your youth pastor or your parents). Then, as you plan and before the event takes place, there's one more very important step to take—a step that might require you to meet a few times before you do this: Pray!

Let's do that right now.

> *Lord God, You are so great! I am eager to plunge deeper into surrender and forgiveness with You. I want to experience the fullness of Your freedom that comes from truly forgiving others. And I want others to know that freedom too. I pray that you'll bless our outreach. Give us creative ideas, wisdom and clarity. Help it to be fun! Above all, I pray that Jesus will be honored in my life, whether at a big event or in the small, secret things that I do each day. I love You! In Jesus' name, amen.*

Note

1. Charles Wesley, "And Can It Be," *Psalms and Hymns*, 1738.